MW01593771

When All Hope Is Gone What Then?

An Anthology

Edited by
Dr. Diane Gross
Annie Louise Twitchell

Copyright © 2025 Dr. Diane Gross

All rights reserved.

Editing: Dr. Diane Gross and Annie Louise Twitchell

Cover Design and Book Layout: Annie Louise Twitchell

Cover Image Editor: Brandon McCormack

Cover Image: Licensed

ISBN: 9798289369482

To those who find themselves without hope. You are not alone.

CONTENTS

ACKNOWLEDGMENTS

To all our dear writers, thank you for sharing your stories.
To all our beloved readers, thank you for reading.

Introduction

Humpty Dumpty sat on a wall.

Humpty Dumpty had a great fall.

All the King's horses

and all the King's men

Couldn't put Humpty together again.

This famous rhyme perfectly depicts what 'when all hope is gone' looks like. Our life feels irreparably broken, and as if there is nothing we or anyone else can do to fix it. We feel powerless.

Humpty Dumpty's tale is the story of the people in this book. The critical issue each person had to answer when their lives and world irrevocably broke into pieces was - what then?

All the accounts in this book are true - told by real people who, at some point, lost all hope. The narratives are raw, honest and at times difficult to read. They are also filled with remarkable courage and strength. A loss of hope can make us feel weak, but it takes enormous fortitude and bravery to continue when you feel like all hope is gone. Surviving loss of hope is not for the faint of heart.

It is important, though, to understand the difference between a wish and real hope. Wishing and hoping for something are both desires for a certain thing or outcome. The vital difference between them is hope is grounded in realistic possibility, while a wish is more rooted in impossible fantasy. Getting caught up in fairytale wishes can steal our joy and make us feel powerless. It can create a sense of grasping and prolonged longing. It can keep us chained to a specific idea of what must happen for our world to be made 'right.' Unrealistic wishing often contributes to a chronic sense of hopelessness.

Recapturing hope, however, is a vital part of surviving brokenness. When there is no way out; around; under; through; or forward - finding hope is essential for navigating such a darkened path. It is the way back to ourselves.

Many of these stories show that sometimes, when all hope is gone, we have to resuscitate it and bring it back to life. This heroic and life-giving act changes us forever. That's what these stories illuminate.

Though loss of hope can make us feel like Humpty Dumpty, unlike him, we can be put back together again - just not in the same form we once were.

The Japanese tradition of Kinsigui, or Kintsukuroi provides powerful imagery of this possibility. This ancient art masterfully uses the broken pieces to create something new and inspiring. Kintsukuroi is the technique of repairing broken pottery with gold or silver lacquer or precious metal - making it 'more beautiful for having been broken.'

These authors are human kintsukuroi. They each picked up the pieces of their broken lives and put them back together again. Sometimes they had help, but the reality is that nobody could do it for them. Their accounts exemplify a kind of hope that holds promise for the future that doesn't rest in happenstance. These stories demonstrate that tapping into and utilizing the powerful resources we have at our disposal - including spiritual, relational, and internal - can help resuscitate and resurrect hope. The kind of hope these authors model provides a roadmap on how to forge a new and different path through the darkness.

Editors Dr. Diane Gross and Annie Louise Twitchell

Sweet Darkness

When your eyes are tired
the world is tired also.

When your vision has gone,
no part of the world can find you.

Time to go into the dark
where the night has eyes
to recognize its own.

There you can be sure
you are not beyond love.

The dark will be your home
tonight.

The night will give you a horizon
further than you can see.

You must learn one thing.
The world was made to be free in.

Give up all the other worlds
except the one to which you belong.

Sometimes it takes darkness and the sweet
confinement of your aloneness
to learn

anything or anyone
that does not bring you alive

is too small for you.

...

'Sweet Darkness'
From 'The House of Belonging'
Poems by David Whyte
© David Whyte and Many Rivers Press

Hope is Coming Home to Yourself

I never expected my marriage to end like this - me, unshowered and weeping, walking down Highway 24, trying to hitchhike home.

The morning light painted the mountains in soft gold, a beauty that felt almost cruel against the terror in my heart. Each passing car sent my pulse racing, each distant rumble of an engine made me wonder if this would be the one to stop, the one to carry me away from everything I was leaving behind.

Ten days earlier, I'd joined my husband on the Colorado Trail with hope blooming in my chest. He'd been hiking for weeks, covering nearly 200 miles of wilderness, and his voice on our intermittent opportunities to touch base carried a peace I hadn't heard in months. "The trail is changing me," he said. "I'm finding myself out here." When he asked me to join him for the final stretch, I thought perhaps we were finding our way back to each other.

The first few days felt like a dream. We walked through alpine meadows scattered with wildflowers, set up camp beneath stars so bright they seemed to pulse. But as the miles stretched on, the dream began to fray at the edges. His criticisms, at first quiet mutters, grew louder. His frustrations, recently constrained, began to spiral.

Somewhere around mile 250, everything shattered. The trail map he was carrying led us to a swamp instead of the expected water source, and his rage erupted like a geyser. He raged all night, screaming at me, throwing things. I slid inside my sleeping bag, hoping night would calm the fury. But morning just brought more. More anger. More insults. More of him telling me that it was all MY fault. He'd been holding the map. He'd been leading the way. But now that we were here, it was SOMEHOW my fault. It was always my fault.

"You're a selfish, stupid, f*cking bitch, you know that?" He spat at me.

I tucked my head down, quieted myself in the hopes that I could quiet him too. But the rage continued.

As he looked at me, soft, bent, and scared, unwilling to engage, he lifted his finger, fiercely pointed at my face, and hissed, "As far as I'm concerned you can f*ck off without me."

And just like that, I felt an awakening. "Okay, I will."

I buckled my pack across my breastbone, stepped back on the dusty trail, and started walking. I started to whisper to myself: "Don't go back. Do not go back, Brooke." Then louder, my voice overcoming his: "Do not go back. You are done being treated like this." As his booming waned behind me, a raven stared at me from the side of the road and cawed, as though joining me in my mantra: Caw. Caw. "Do not go back. Do not go back."

For hours, I walked along the highway with trembling courage, trying to decide which of the passing cars I could trust. The sun climbed higher, the morning grew warmer, and still I walked. When I spotted a couple pulled off at a scenic overlook near Leadville, my heart caught in my throat. I sucked in a breath of air; tried to calm my sobs; tried to smooth my wild hair; to appear less desperate than I felt. But the tears came anyway, spilling down my unwashed face as I stood several feet away, hoping to appear safe: "Please, I'm so sorry, I just...I just hitchhiked away from my husband. He is dangerous and I—"

The woman turned to look at me, and what I saw in her eyes nearly broke me. Not pity, not judgment, but a deep, knowing kindness. "Sweet girl," she said, her voice warm and steady, "we just dropped our child off at college and we have this whole day to do anything we want. We will take you anywhere. We will take you anywhere you want to go. Let's just get you safe."

Those words—let's just get you safe—opened something in me I hadn't even known was locked. As they drove down the mountain, she lovingly kept turning to make sure I was okay. She asked no questions but offered something far more valuable: the gift of being seen and believed.

In the months that followed, I learned that leaving is both an ending and a beginning. The path of healing has been neither straight nor simple. Some days I felt like a warrior, others like a ghost of myself. I had to relearn trust—not just of others, but to trust my own heart. I had to understand that strength isn't measured by how much you can endure, but by how honestly you can love yourself.

Slowly, like spring after a long winter, I began to grow into a new version of myself. The woman who had spent years making herself smaller, quieter, more acceptable began to unfurl. I found my voice again, first in whispers, then in stories shared with others who had walked similar paths. These stories became the heart of what I do now, hosting the Good Mama Magic podcast, where I explore the quiet miracles of finding our way back to ourselves.

What I've learned about hope is this: it doesn't always announce itself with fanfare. Sometimes it arrives in the smallest moments—in a stranger's kindness, in the courage to take one step and then another, in the quiet certainty that rises from your bones when you finally choose yourself. Hope lives in the understanding that you carry everything you need within you, that even when you feel most lost, you're on your way to being found.

That morning on Highway 24 wasn't just an escape. It was a return—to myself, to truth, to the understanding that home isn't a place or a person, but a feeling of rightness in your own skin. It's the knowledge that no matter where the road leads, you can trust your feet to carry you, your heart to guide you, your spirit to light the way.

Now, when I look back at that morning, I see more than just the end of my marriage. I see the beginning of a journey home—not to any particular place, but to the quiet certainty that lives in my own heart. It's a truth that keeps unfolding: no matter where you are, no matter how far you've wandered, you can always come home to yourself. Sometimes the longest journey is the one that leads you right back to your own heart, where you discover that everything you needed was within you all along. And somehow, in the gentle unfolding of this new life, I've found that home was never really lost at all. It was waiting, patient as mountains, for me to find my way back to myself.

Brooke Lark

"Hope is the thing with feathers."

Emily Dickenson

Unseeable Light

"You are going to become blind, so start practicing getting around now."

Though this wasn't an actual voice I heard as I descended the darkened staircase that morning, this internal 'knowing' was something with which I was quite familiar. It doesn't happen often, but I have experienced a number of these intuitive revelations in my life, all of which have come true. As a result, I was not quick to simply dismiss it.

I began to practice. For a couple of years, I practiced walking downstairs with my eyes closed. I learned to count steps. Other times I deliberately didn't count, instead trying to get a sense of when the last step was approaching. When I took my morning walks, I practiced walking with my eyes closed. I tried to increase the number of steps I took before I started to feel an overwhelming need to open my eyes to check my position. I performed a variety of tasks with my eyes closed, often making a game of it.

I knew, even before it happened, but I still wasn't fully prepared for when it did.

Once it started, my eyes quickly worsened. In the beginning, they felt so strained and tired it became difficult to keep them open.

Over the next few months, it began to feel as if I had an eyelash under my eyelids all the time. This quickly progressed to a constant sensation of gravel and ground glass. It was extremely painful. My eyes began to reflexively blink nonstop. Sometimes too, it felt as though one or both of my eyeballs were shriveling up in my head.

Though I wasn't considered legally blind because my acuity was not yet severely affected, I was functionally blind. I could no longer do many of the things that had previously been an integral part of my life. I couldn't read, which had always been a great love of mine. I couldn't write, which was how I often processed my world. I couldn't edit the last book I had written. I couldn't drive, which meant I was often homebound. I wasn't able to engage with people on social media with any frequency. I began to avoid in-person social interactions because it was so taxing. A significant way in which I had always connected with people was through eye contact and reading body language. These essential tools for how I gauged and adjusted to the tenor of my interactions were substantially impacted.

My world shrunk dramatically.

Over the next few years, several eye doctors treated me. Their initial diagnosis was severe dry eye disease. However, I didn't respond to even the most innovative treatments for dry eye. Eventually more intensive testing revealed my severe dry eyes were a symptom, not the root cause of my eye issues. I had an underlying condition that had been missed. As time went on many of the lubricating glands in my eyes became scarred, depriving my eyes of much needed moisture. The severity of dryness resulted in abscesses on the surface of my eyes and corneas.

I was functionally blind, since I had to keep my eyes closed most of the time due to the constant and excruciating pain.

Over the next year I underwent a total of five surgeries. With each surgery, I clung to the hope my eyes would get better. That did not happen. I was despondent and consumed by fear. The idea of spending the rest of my life in pain and with severe visual functional impairment was devastating. I wanted to die.

This emotional period of darkness lasted about four days. Then, I had a moment of clarity. I suddenly realized I could focus on my limitations, or I could focus on ways to do things I love. Many people before me, with far worse visual impairments - in some cases total blindness - lived joyful, meaningful lives. Many have even changed the world. I realized my challenge was to also find a way to live a life of joy and contribution.

I thought about the impact of people like Helen Keller, Andrea Bocelli, Stevie Wonder, Joseph Pulitzer, Galileo, Monet, and Harriet Tubman. Their examples inspired me and left me without excuses. I decided I could wallow or follow. I could wallow in my pain and misery, remaining mired in feeling helpless, or I could follow the example of their courage.

So, I considered how to continue to do the things I loved, even if nothing changed with my eyes. I spoke with the companies for whom I had provided workshops and webinars for decades. They offered to provide a Communications Facilitator for every webinar I taught for them to provide support by assisting me with tasks my eyes would not allow me to do. I developed strategies to continue to provide some services to my patients. I *listened* to my favorite movies. I 'read' via audio books. I now utilize a ride service for people with disabilities. I travel internationally with my sister, arranging for special accommodation as needed. I hired two editors to finish editing the book that had been languishing for almost three years. I put in place the resources necessary to compile the book you're reading right now. And I started working with a therapist to help me process the enormous impact my visual impairment has had on my life.

In short, I decided to live with purpose and joy instead of waiting and praying for death.

At this point, I am still unable to drive. I can read for a few minutes now, but my eyes quickly become strained, so I still depend heavily on audio versions of information. I can, however, keep my eyes open more, which has made day-to-day activities much easier. I have to get regular treatments designed to calm the eye spasms that became hardwired due to blinking so much, for so long. While the discomfort is still constant, I take solace in the fact that the pain is no longer excruciating.

Sometimes I still feel overwhelmed by my limitations. In those moments, I seek to treat myself with tenderness and compassion. I honestly don't know if my eyes will ever return to anything resembling normal, but regardless of what happens, I am committed to living my best life.

My mantra has become a line I heard in a movie a few years ago - "The most important light is the light we cannot see." This inclusive, larger light has expanded my world dimensionally. I am learning to access and trust my insight and deeper intuition more skillfully. I see the value of nurturing a rich internal world, not just an external one. And while I can more easily see through façades, pretenses, and inauthenticity, I also see kindness, empathy, generosity, courage and other intangible qualities in myself and others much more readily.

This unseeable light has illuminated much beauty in life I had previously missed seeing. It has given me the gift of greater insight. It has certainly shown me that real hope isn't predicated on getting a specific, desired outcome. There are, after all, some things beyond our ability to control. Hope, rather, is an active response to life's difficulties. It is a choice to believe in and work toward a positive outcome, despite adversity. It's a way of engaging with life's challenges with optimism and positive action to create a brighter future.

You see - hope is an unseeable light.

Diane Gross

"Because what's worse than knowing you want something, besides knowing you can never have it?"

James Patterson, The Angel Experiment

The Decision

Dread. I didn't know what that word meant at the time, but looking back I see how utterly hopeless my life felt from my earliest memory. My family situation looked normal from the outside, happy even, however that image was the furthest thing from the truth. On the surface, I had what every 90's kid dreamed of. I had two non-divorced parents, a home, all the toys I could ask for, cable tv, and I got all A's in school. There were no overt or observable signs of abuse or neglect. But from a very young age I felt a sense of deep dread and persistent nervousness. No matter how "smart," or "good" people told me I was, I felt constantly unsure of myself, ineffective, and in some important but hard to describe way I felt out of control. I was often labelled shy, but what really was taking place was a lack of consistent or reliable space for my own emotions or developing sense of self. That space was often taken up by another. Someone who over-mothered and over-controlled.

I always felt like my biological mother treated me like a 'lap creature' or pet. She wanted me to sit on her lap and love her endlessly. Her favorite place to be, both literally and emotionally, was as close to her as possible. She normalized it to such an extent that I was still regularly sitting on her lap when I was thirteen years old. I felt a faint but distinct sense of shame about it, but when a primary caregiver normalizes and rewards a behavior, it can be hard to identify the confusing emotions around it. I knew something about it was 'off,' but it was all that I knew. She treated me like an infant in a variety of other ways. I didn't learn many of the basic skills one might expect of a young, prepubescent boy. I was taught to depend on her to do the simplest things for me, like peeling my bananas, or opening an umbrella. It was a manipulative method of controlling me. If she could keep me helpless, unsure, and unskilled, then I would have to remain dependent on her. It would ensure that I would stay close to her and continue to provide her with the attention and love she craved. Life perpetually revolved around her unmet emotional needs. My larger function or purpose was to provide emotional regulation for someone else, instead of learning how to regulate my own.

My father was autistic. He was a hard worker, but sheer emotional connection with him was challenging. It always felt like he too was just a means to an end for her. He brought in a good salary, provided a nice home - and was easily controlled and compliant. Despite her emotional volatility and tendencies toward control, she knew he would do what he needed to do and never leave. I love him deeply and miss him every day (he passed away in 2020), but I also recognize that he did not provide significant support, structure, or parenting, and that he was in certain ways as influenced by these dynamics as I was.

I was prescribed my first antidepressant medication when I was five years old after the doctor noticed I was small for my age, pale, and lethargic. Essentially, I was failing to thrive. I had consistent headaches and stomachaches, manifestations of my constant tension and fear. Nothing was actually wrong with me, though, that healthier family dynamics couldn't fix. They diagnosed me with a chemical imbalance, but they never bothered to explore what might have caused such an imbalance in a five-year-old child. By the time I was thirteen, the list of medications I was on had climbed to twelve. Some were for side-effects, and others for side-effects of the side-effects. The medications helped me comply and be 'good Nicky'.

I was smart. I started reading at a very early age and excelled in school. That was a bragging point for my biological mother. My level of intelligence and how people viewed me was important to her. Any attempt on my part to have my own identity was punished. So, I was expected to be a 'good boy' - a perfect kid so that she would look good. I tried. But it was a lot of pressure, and my anxiety was constant and palpable. I felt like my world was perpetually out of control.

Then came puberty, the time of differentiation. Adolescence is the time when children are supposed to develop a more solid sense of self-identity and self-worth. It's when they tend to learn at a deeper level to regulate their own emotions, instead of relying on others to do so. My ability to do any of that was massively depressed. My development up until that time had been severely impeded. I had become a dependent 'lump.' Puberty was a time of enormous turmoil because I was undergoing intense hormonal and cognitive changes, I didn't have the foundation or skill sets to handle. I couldn't connect with others because I couldn't even connect with myself.

I wanted to die. I considered suicide, but had watched my biological mother try - and fail numerous times. It wasn't pretty. I was too afraid to attempt it. My fear was colored with feeling ashamed that I couldn't even do that right. I felt unable to even end my own life.

I felt powerless - and hopeless.

Then, something unexpected happened. The day started off horribly. My second cousin was getting married and my biological mother wanted me there, so I became an unwilling guest. But that's the day I met who would eventually become my new mother - Diane. She had flown in from New York to attend the wedding.

She had what I describe to people as a 'good vibe.' She felt like a much more grounded, centered person than I had previously experienced. It's hard to explain, but I could tell she was a good person who cared about people. We ended up having a conversation. My memories of what we talked about are blurry, since I was heavily medicated, but I do remember she seemed to legitimately want to help me. Nobody had ever tried to help me before - not the doctors; not the teachers; not my family; not the psychiatrist. They just all seemed invested in trying to control my behaviors and keep me compliant. She listened to me, and I sensed no desire on her part to control me.

Over the next eighteen months I regularly called Diane. We just talked. I grew more and more convinced that she cared about me. I felt seen and heard. I felt validated as a worthwhile person.

As my eighth-grade year progressed, I started experiencing agoraphobic tendencies. I panicked at the thought of leaving the house. I absolutely refused to go to school. I just couldn't do it all anymore. I couldn't do anything. I began to wonder if death was better and would fantasize about the relief it might bring. But even suicidal ideation further emphasized how ineffective I felt, because I was too limited by fear and inability to even act on that. I felt like I had zero purpose or ability, and ultimately I felt I was going to die unless something massively changed. But some deeper wisdom inside me also knew that I would never be able to make the changes I wanted to while remaining in my current home. I instinctively knew that I would never be able to change if I continued to live there. I knew that I could not fight my environment and thought that maybe I would stand a chance if I was in a more supportive place.

This understanding led me to what I call, The Decision. I remember every detail about it. I remember the exact time, the colors in the room, and the sound of my heartbeat as I pulled out our fake red leather contact book to get Diane's telephone number. Then I dialed her number: "Hello, Diane? This is Nick. I wanted to ask you the biggest favor that anyone could possibly ask. Is there any way that I could come and live with you?" She told me I could, and that she actually had known from the beginning that I would eventually come live with them. That response deeply encouraged me and convinced me this was the right decision.

The decision to leave was my first real behavioral shift. I tended to believe I didn't deserve to take up space in the world, yet here I was asking for her and her husband, Richard, to make space for me. It was an enormous step.

I did and said whatever I had to convince my biological mother to let me go. She agreed. I think she believed it would be temporary since I never stuck with anything for very long. I was content to let her believe that. June 4, 2004, I flew to New York, and on July 18, 2004, a judge awarded legal guardianship to Diane and Richard. It wasn't until I was an adult, however, that I finally asked them if I could call them 'mom' and 'dad.' They were thrilled for me to do so.

After I moved, my life underwent a series of massive changes. I immediately, almost effortlessly, dropped weight. I had been significantly overweight from lack of movement and as a side effect of medication. I was able to have a conversation without falling asleep, since the medications were revisited, and I was subsequently weaned off them. My chronic bed wetting also went away.

And I began to find myself.

Their approach to parenting me made an enormous difference. Gone was the clingy, infantilizing approach to which I had become accustomed. Diane and Richard focused on helping me develop and grow skills I needed to live a successful and happy life. They wanted to help me learn to think and be independent. One story that exemplifies their approach is when I decided to explore the wooded area behind the house. It didn't go well. I fell into a lake, got eaten up by mosquitoes and got lost. I ended up coming out of the woods a few miles away, but I couldn't remember our address or the phone number. I knocked on a stranger's door and asked for help. They drove me around until I recognized the house. When I got back home, I made the comment, "Man - I'm never going back out there again!" I was too afraid. Diane looked me squarely in the face and said, "You know, if you avoid doing things just because you're afraid, or it didn't work out perfectly, your world will start to shrink. What if instead, you think about how you can do it smarter and safer next time?"

That changed my approach to life. I wanted to expand my world. I realized I had spent a lifetime running away from discomfort and things that scared me. I slowly began to understand that true freedom happens when we learn to move toward things, even discomfort. The decision to love yourself in general, is at its core, moving toward ourselves. And for most of us, it involves moving through various levels of pain and discomfort to get there. It's only when we are willing to face our fear and our pain that we can transform it, and ourselves. Over the next several years I continued to engage with different learning experiences and challenges, but with a desire to learn and grow from them so that they could expand my world, not take away from it.

Today, at thirty-four years old, my life is a dream, rather than the nightmare I had imagined when I was a young child. I have parents and siblings who love me. I have an amazing group of supportive and wonderful friends. I am in a relationship with an amazing man who I deeply love. I am a Doctor of Clinical Psychology and Assistant Director of a large clinical practice. I have the privilege to help other people as they work on their own healing.

Decisions are powerful. Particularly the decision to love yourself. They may require the courage to take risks, but they also can be life changing. My decision certainly changed mine.

Nickolas Armstrong

Life Was One Big Headache

I am a 71-year-old man in generally good health, though I have been plagued by migraine headaches for years. The pain from migraines has been so intense and debilitating at times that it robs me of my ability to think or act rationally, sometimes relegating other, more serious health issues to the backseat.

The first headache I can clearly recall was on a cold, wintry Sunday in February 1961, when I was seven years old. I was in the second grade. It was the first time I was allowed to go sledding down my favorite sliding hill without my parents. I went with a sixth-grade neighbor friend. I remember happily carrying my sled to the top of the hill and flying down the hill in gleeful abandon!

Suddenly, a toboggan laden with four or five people slammed into me. The collision was so violent that I lost consciousness. The incident got the attention of a few adults, who immediately rushed to my assistance. I recall feeling incredibly confused about what had happened. People kept asking if I was all right, and if I needed to be driven home. But in the end, my friend walked me home.

That was the beginning of my long and very painful journey with migraines. When I got home, my mother put me to bed with a cool washcloth on my forehead. My head hurt so badly! I was confused and disoriented. The pain in my head was still so severe the next day that I couldn't even go to school. I was, however, able to return to school the second day after the accident. After that, the headache dissipated and did not return for a number of years.

It is unclear whether that collision is the reason for my future migraines, however, I began to have regular and debilitating migraines when I was twelve years old. Looking back, I wonder if the onset was related to the fact that I was going through puberty, and the corresponding hormonal changes my body was experiencing. The cause of the migraines is still officially unknown.

I don't remember ever receiving medical attention when I was young. It may be because the initial migraines I experienced at twelve years of age only lasted for a few months, and then occurred only intermittently. Over the next few years, the intensity and frequency began to escalate. By the time I was in eleventh grade, they had become so horrendous that my parents took me to the doctor. The doctor prescribed some medication that is commonly used to treat tension headaches. This treatment was quite effective at the time to help relieve those painful episodes.

I experienced some respite from migraines in my twenties, and on the rare occurrence I did have one, an over-the-counter pain reliever seemed adequate.

In my thirties I began to have regular migraines that were so painful they would bring me to my knees. I would have stabbing, intense pain behind one of my eyes that radiated throughout my entire head. Thankfully, I did not suffer from nausea or vomiting as do many migraine sufferers, nor did I see auras often experienced by some. I did experience severe photophobia, however, which is an intense sensitivity to light with my migraines. I needed to be in a dark room to mitigate some of the pain that I was experiencing. The migraines were often debilitating and lasted four to five hours. I often felt like I wanted to die during these excruciating episodes. Though I never had suicidal thoughts the pain has often been so intense that I have been driven to think darkly.

For me, migraines have sometimes been dark times, in a dark room, with dark thoughts. This has been challenging, to say the least.

Because my life was being consumed by pain, I became obsessed with anything that might help me. I was told certain foods were triggers. I experimented but could never identify a food trigger for my migraines. Well-meaning friends and coworkers would often suggest various treatments. This could be frustrating, especially if the treatments were things I had already tried! One friend insisted that all I needed was to take magnesium. However, I was already taking it. Nothing I did seemed to help.

The whole situation began to feel hopeless!

I began to experience increasingly severe migraines in my

forties, fifties, and sixties - and still into my seventies. I was treated by a neurologist with a variety of drugs to try to control, and hopefully prevent, my migraines. Eventually, I was given two options to try to prevent migraines from occurring at all. I could use a potent migraine medication, or I could get Botox injections every 90 days. I opted for Botox injections.

The frequency of my migraines at that time was 17 to 18 times a month. With Botox the frequency decreased to 7 to 8 times a month, which was certainly an improvement, though not a cure. I was still suffering a great deal, and it was impacting my life and ability to function at a significant level. In addition to the Botox, I eventually was prescribed a new drug that was supposed to be very effective at aborting migraines once they began. The relief I got was amazing! It stopped my migraines within an hour of taking the medication. The problem was I could only take nine tablets a month. After I had two strokes, however, I had to completely stop taking it.

I was discouraged and frustrated. I felt desperate because migraines had come to dominate my life. I had tried so many things, and now the one thing that had worked best was something I had to give up. My neurologist told me most patients eventually outgrow their migraines, then he briefly paused, and said, "but you were my oldest patient."

Once again, I tried everything I could think of. I even used an opioid prescribed by my neurologist. I tried six weeks of acupuncture, but to no avail. I went for deep tissue massages, which helped my lower back issues and my neck and shoulders but did not help my migraines. I even asked my son to research what type of cannabis would help migraines. I tried it, but it provided no relief for me. I research natural products that sometimes seem to help prevent migraines. I used a variety of natural supplements that the American Migraine Foundation, the American Headache Society, and the FDA all found could be helpful. I had taken all those supplements for fifteen years, so I decided to experiment with dosages. I did find that those natural approaches at higher dosages seemed to help substantially reduce, and at times even eliminate, my migraines.

My journey with migraines has been a long and painful one. At the beginning of this year, the number of migraines I had diminished considerably. I have not had to get Botox injections since October 2023. I know, however, that it is an option if my migraines recur. I am still not headache free, but I now have a specific routine that seems to help if I feel a migraine coming on.

Am I healed? No. But I am grateful to be living with much less pain nowadays. I always encourage people with any illness to seek professional medical assistance - and to never stop looking for an answer! Pain can drive people to extremes, so we often need the support of people who are experienced in dealing with whatever it is we are facing. It has made an enormous difference in my life. And I am so thankful to have arrived at a much better and less painful time in my life.

It has been a long journey to get here!

Bill Hesser

Through Hope and Despair

October 24, 2022, is a day deeply etched into my memory. My wife, Anna Lee, was gripped by severe chest pain, compelling us to seek emergency care at Southland Hospital, where she was diagnosed with pneumonia. After being treated, and when the pain subsided, we returned home, only to be forced to return the following day because her agonizing pain intensified. Painkillers proved effective and she was sent home once again. Then, a call from the doctor later that afternoon changed everything! We were informed that cancer cells had been detected in her blood. Anna Lee had leukemia. This was the underlying cause of her pneumonia.

In that moment, our lives were irrevocably altered forever. Two days later, with a heavy heart, I followed my wife's ambulance to Dunedin Hospital where she was to start her treatment. The care of our two daughters was relegated to friends and family as I struggled with the weight of the new reality we faced.

Upon arrival at the hospital, the hematologist's diagnosis of acute lymphoblastic leukemia (ALL) struck me like a thunderclap! The doctor's explanations were a blur as I wept uncontrollably. My mind was overwhelmed with a flood of all the dire possibilities that might loom ahead. Despite the medical team's reassurances, the sense of anxiety was enormous.

After a few days, Anna Lee's recovery from pneumonia allowed me to briefly return to work. Every weekend I traveled to Dunedin to visit her. This took a toll on my physical and emotional health. The sense of isolation I experienced was stark compared to the communal support I had known while growing up in the Philippines. There, family and friends would rally around a loved one in need. Now, I simply felt isolated and alone.

As I was grappling with all these challenges, my faith was also being sorely tested. As a Catholic, I found myself questioning the reason for our suffering. The Cancer Society provided invaluable support, helping me navigate the depths of depression and the emotional strains of this ordeal. But I must admit, it was disheartening when people only inquired about my wife's condition, leaving my own struggles unacknowledged. I felt invisible.

On the night of December 31, 2023, Anna Lee was able to celebrate New Year's with us, despite my reservations because of her condition. My instincts urged me to keep her in the hospital, but her eagerness to be with us prevailed. Early on January 1, 2024, however, I had to rush her back to the hospital because she developed a high fever. Her condition deteriorated rapidly, and she was admitted to the ICU. My brother-in-law took our daughters to Christchurch so that I could focus on what was happening with my wife. This support was a bittersweet relief. Still, it again left me with a profound sense of loneliness.

After the harrowing ICU experience and a grueling series of chemotherapy sessions, our lives took another turn on February 27, 2023. We moved to Christchurch for Anna Lee's bone marrow transplant, a critical step in her battle against leukemia. My work at the Southern Institute of technology graciously permitted me to work remotely so that I could be with her. This move, though essential, brought a whirlwind of change and challenges that tested every fiber of my being. Leaving behind our home and relocating to Ranui House, an accommodation for bone marrow transplant patients, was a monumental adjustment for our entire family. Our children had to adjust to a new school, and they missed their friends and familiar surroundings. I found myself struggling with the weight of this upheaval while trying to maintain some semblance of normalcy. Every day presented a new struggle, and the physical and emotional toll of our circumstances felt overwhelming.

Our proximity to our brother-in-law's family had the potential to have offered a high-level of support, but sadly it resulted instead in a series of misunderstandings. The stress that enveloped everyone led to tensions that were sometimes difficult to navigate. I felt an acute sense of isolation as their reactions seemed to reflect a lack of understanding of our unique struggles. Their inability to empathize in the way I needed, added to my own mounting stress, and compounded the psychological, emotional, and physical strains I was already enduring. The sense of alienation was profound. During our stay in Christchurch, I continued to teach online. This was both a lifeline and an added burden. Balancing my professional responsibilities with the demand of caring for my wife and managing our family life was overwhelming. The need to please Anna Lee's family and, at the same time, ensure her care was maintained became my greatest challenge. Each day was a battle to allay emotional exhaustion and the relentless cycle of hope and despair.

In July 2023, after her bone marrow transplant treatment, we returned home. Anna Lee's parents joined us from the Philippines to help. We hoped returning home would bring some semblance of stability and comfort; however, our optimism was soon overshadowed by the grim reality of graft-versus-host disease (GVHD). This condition sometimes occurs when donor bone marrow or stem cells attack the recipient. It can cause myriad symptoms, including systemic pain, skin issues, gastrointestinal distress, mouth, ulcers, and more. For Anna Lee, it caused immense suffering. Her condition deteriorated daily. Our lives were transformed into a relentless cycle of emergency department visits, hospital, wards, and moments at home.

The emotional toll of watching my wife's health decline, despite all efforts, was crushing. Each setback eroded my hope. I struggled to reconcile her worsening condition with my desire to remain optimistic and strong for her sake. The constant whiplash between hope and despair was exhausting. I often found myself on the brink of giving up! This was especially difficult when Anna Lee placed the needs of others above her own, which came at a cost to her own health, as well as to our well-being as a family.

In those darkest moments, I struggled with feelings of

inadequacy and helplessness. The strain of maintaining a façade of strength, while internally questioning whether I was doing enough, was a heavy burden to bear. It was difficult to balance my role as a caretaker, a parent, and a husband - all while navigating the complexities of our shifting family dynamics.

Through this turbulent journey, the trials we faced were not just physical, but deeply emotional. The hope that had fueled our fight began to wane as each new complication arose. Yet the love and commitment we shared continued to be a source of strength. It was this unwavering devotion that carried us through the darkest hours, reminding us that even in the midst of profound suffering, the bounds of our love and family remained unbreakable.

On June 12, 2024, our world shifted once again when Anna Lee was airlifted to another hospital that was better equipped to deal with her rapidly deteriorating and fragile condition. The helicopter sliced through the sky, carrying not just her frail body, but also the weight of our shared hopes and fears. Her sepsis had worsened. It was terrifying! When I saw her in the emergency room, my heart felt as though it was being crushed under the unbearable weight of despair. I could not contain my tears. Yet, even while I sobbed, she turned to me with a frail smile, and said, "Bakit ka umiiyak? Hindi pa naman ako patay?" ("Why are you crying? I am not dead yet.") Her words, though intended to comfort, only increased the ache in my chest.

Two days later, on June 14, 2024, her condition significantly worsened. The hematologist, their faces etched with concern, informed me that her sepsis was severe, and that her chances of survival were slim. They advised me to gather our family for a final farewell while she was still conscious. Their words felt like a cruel twist of fate, a harsh reminder that hope was slipping through our fingers.

I made the heart-wrenching calls to family members. But even as I spoke the words, the finality of the situation did not fully sink in. I continued to cling to the belief she might still recover. It was a desperate hope against the encroaching darkness I sought to escape.

The following day her condition deteriorated further. She was rushed to the ICU and connected to a ventilator to aid her breathing. She was administered antibiotics in large doses. But as each day passed, her situation grew more desperate. The antibiotics seemed completely ineffective against the advancing sepsis. On June 18, 2024, the medical team suggested that, at this stage, providing her with comfort care rather than continued treatment would be more compassionate. I was initially resistant, hoping against hope that one more day might make a difference. But after a poignant conversation with my father-in-law, who gently advised me to consider letting her go, I began to confront the painful truth. I realized that her suffering needed to end. The ventilator, though keeping her alive, was causing her distress and discomfort. The weight of all the pain, grief, and love came crashing down. I let myself weep for what felt like an eternity.

June 19, 2024, was an incredibly sad day. As the time for the ventilator removal approached, I gathered with relatives and close friends for a final goodbye. The atmosphere was thick with sorrow, and the moment felt suspended in heart wrenching stillness. At 4:37 PM my beloved wife, Anna Lee, was declared dead. I felt devastated. The plans we had made, the promises we had exchanged and all the dreams we held for the future were irrevocably and forever lost.

In those final moments, I realized the depth of her bravery. She was not just a fighter against leukemia, but an extraordinary person in every sense. She was a loving mother, a devoted wife, a cherished daughter, and a steadfast friend. Though Anna Lee did not "win" her battle against or survive leukemia - she won a much harder battle. She had stood on the battleground against cancer with courage, grace, and kindness. She is an inspiration to every cancer patient fighting for their lives!

Anna Lee will forever live in my heart. She gave me two wonderful daughters, and despite her suffering, was always humble and selfless. Allowing me to shine gave her immense joy. Her strength and spirit were cornerstones of my own achievements! I'll be forever grateful.

I am still processing Anna Lee's death and struggling with intense grief. The pain of her absence is a constant companion and reminder of the void in my life. And while I'm still not sure her family fully understands the depths of the struggle she and I faced; I hope one day they will.

Now I awaken each day with a renewed sense of purpose. My purpose is my two daughters! They are the beacons of light in the dark. They are the reason I get out of bed each morning. Their laughter, their curiosity, and their innocent smiles offer a wellspring of inspiration and motivation. They motivate me to forge ahead. I know that in my wife's absence, I will need to be there for my daughters to provide support in ways that my wife will not be here to offer. They will need me to be there for significant milestones in their lives - like their first menstruation, their debuts, their graduations and one day, their weddings. I am determined and committed to being fully present for them!

My hope in sharing my story is that it will help people recognize that those who are suffering and dying are not the only ones in need of support. Those who support and care for them and witness their suffering do as well! Their pain, though less visible, is very real. They too need understanding, compassion, and support. They certainly do not need judgment or criticism in their time of distress. Compassion and empathy can foster a more supportive and caring environment and community. When we extend understanding and kindness in this way, we honor the enduring strength and love that binds us all, even during our darkest moments.

I love you Ma, and I always will…

Carlo Mateo Gabriel

Schoosmunchchuck (Someone Special)

I often call my son Schoosmunchchuck. I was reading
Sacajawea when I was pregnant with him. She was pregnant when she
guided Lewis and Clark, and she called her unborn child
Skoosmunchchuck, which means "someone special."

Jean-Paul (JP) was born in 1980. The year my father died. The
year John Lennon died. The year we moved into the oldest house in
Durham. He was born with an inch long, light brown mark on his
stomach. We told him it meant he was indeed someone special.

JP had blond hair with streaks of gold. He had light blue
crystalline eyes, which punctuated an undeniable and mysterious energy
he emanated. Objects around him seemed to strangely respond to his
touch. If he touched a thermostat, the spring would pop out. If he
touched the needle on the record player, it would break. Once I saw
him reach his little hand high above his head to touch the adding
machine on the table above him. The whole machine went crazy! The
keys began to wildly pop out in all directions, their heads bobbing and
dancing at the top of their springs like a scene from Fantasia.

This intense energy didn't always manifest in benign ways.
Sometimes it would seem to suddenly explode out of his being. One

moment, for example, he would be playing peacefully with his sister, Jenny, and then suddenly slap her face.

He began to have frequent and uncontrollable temper tantrums.

JP was a surprise. I have often wondered if my emotional trauma from the death of my father, the move, and the belief that I might now have to give up my dream of going to law school negatively impacted him in the womb.

Jean-Paul is a sweet man. JP laughs often and easily. When he was a baby, I would run upstairs thinking that he was crying only to see that he was laughing. Sweet, sparkling faery laughter.

We often cuddled in front of the fireplace. We still do. He and I take nature walks together. He loves the earth, plants, birds, and water.

As time passed, JPs flares of temper increased. When he was six years old, I took him to a therapist. She began to teach us how to help him. We looked him in the eyes and told him we loved him, and that we loved being with him. But he turned his head and said, "No, I'm a bad boy." We were shocked because we never used those words with our children. We purposefully addressed behavior when we corrected them rather than shame their personhood. As time went on he did not turn away from the love.

With the therapist's guidance, we began to incorporate 'five minutes quiet time out' into our parenting. As I held him, if JP could stay quiet and in control for five minutes, he learned he would be released from time-out. If he continued raging, pounding his head against me and screaming, the five minutes started over. He watched the time on the clock Giving him control. This really seemed to help quell his emotional storms.

As we held his gaze, it seemed as if JP began to accept love more easily. But he was still unpredictable. It was mysterious to me that he could rage one moment, then be calm and sweet when he was in time-out.

I hoped he would grow out of this. I wished he could always be in time out.

I sometimes blamed myself for his emotional struggles. I had my own issues with guilt, low self-esteem, and anger. I hadn't been taught how to deal with emotions, so how could I teach my child? I did the best I could, but it is hard to overcome the low self-esteem of a lifetime. Much later, I wrote him letters taking responsibility for my failures as a parent due to my issues.

My therapist believed I was angry at my mother for not giving me love. My mother was often critical, discounting, and dismissive of me.

I felt worthless. I felt like I didn't have the right to even breathe.

I think because of my own experience with my mother, I was determined my children would know they were special and could do anything they dreamed. We wanted to make sure they knew their voice and opinions mattered. They were allowed to speak their minds, even about our parenting decisions. We tried to make them feel heard and valued. I often told JP that he was the 'apple of my eye.'

As my son reached his twenties, he started partying, doing drugs, and drinking. His rages worsened. My husband, Bruce, and I would take turns dealing with his outbursts. We relied on each other's support.

Once, he brought two friends to dinner, but I did not have enough food for unexpected company. I asked him in the future to tell me if he planned to invite someone to dinner so that I could make enough food. He went into a rage. Later he started dancing gaily around the fire, asking us to join him in his joy. The painful dissonance I experienced in that moment was overwhelming.

My stomach would often roil when I heard his car drive up. I never knew if he would be in a good mood, or storm inside, screaming at us and slamming doors.

When he was in his twenties, he had a family meeting to tell us he was gay. He always told me how much our love meant to him. He related the horror of gay friends' parents disowning them.

In 2007 I nearly died from pneumonia. While I was ill, Jenny came in and asked if I needed help. I said, "Well there are dishes in the sink. You know how guys don't notice things like that." Suddenly Jean-Paul was leaning down towards my face on the bed raging at me. He screamed, "you c#*t." I sobbed and sobbed. I couldn't even talk. I struggled for breath. I was shattered. I felt completely helpless and hopeless. Later we talked about the impact of this word on me, and he hasn't called me names since.

One morning, in St. Croix, JP was suddenly raging at me when we started talking about protestors at Pride Parades. "I guess we can't talk about this." I responded, "oh, Jean-Paul." Sighing, I went into my room. While I feel sadness, I have finally come to a place where I am not shattered. The pain is softened. I don't hate myself. I can love us both.

I do still wish we could have had a full discussion of free speech as the Constitution is sacred to me. I also wanted to invite him to come walk with me in the Greensboro Pride.

JP does want to resolve his anger control issues. In the past he has acknowledged the need to do the work. I have tried to help and support him as best I could. I gave him a few books addressing emotions and anger. He said he would read them; however, he returned them unread. He said he would go to therapy, but only went two times.

I know that I can't do his healing work for him - only he can. Some of that work may be accomplished in ways that I don't anticipate or see happening under the surface. He does take the alternate path in most things just as Bruce and I do.

As an adult, Jean-Paul has become involved in several spiritual circles. This has become an important part of his own healing journey. He cares deeply about people. He has volunteered for various organizations, including working at the Human Service Alliance (HSA) with me, in their four-bedroom hospice. One man was having trouble transitioning. JP lovingly held his hand, gazing deeply into his eyes. The man peacefully died the next morning. The staff told us that they believe JP's presence made the difference in the patient's ease of passing.

My son and I share a deep love and joy of music, dancing, and community. This too is part of his healing work. When we attend The Shakori Music Festival, many people stop to hug Jean-Paul and me. They tell me how much they love him and thank me for blessing their lives with him.

It is essential to know that JP is not his rage. He does experience rage, but rage is not who he is. He is so much more than that. He is a person who loves deeply, gives open-heartedly, and is profoundly courageous. In so many ways I am humbled by him.

I admire that he lives his dreams. He travels and follows his adventurous spirit. He has even provided tours for others who want to see other places and countries. He truly is a world citizen. He doesn't let borders or walls limit him. He has become part of a worldwide community, with networks like trees, their roots connected and grounded in love.

He is a cultivator of beauty. As I walk near our home, there is so much flora that Jean-Paul planted and nurtured - daffodils, peonies, and iris including my beloved black iris. Anything he plants does well.

He recently told me that he is now ready to be untethered in the world. He said, "You set me up in so many ways. You told me to live my life and not wait until retirement." He said, "you allowed me to be who I was. I have gratitude all the time."

Now he has plans for a world trip.

JP and I have texted love and support for each other for a long while. He is the child who always asks about me. He is thoughtful, often texting me to check in. He has never ghosted me.

A huge step in my healing occurred because of something my healer and teacher, Fan Ping Tao said to me as I processed some emotional pain about JP. "He is ill," he said. "There is nothing you can do that will change that."

This may sound like a harsh judgment, or like a hopeless

pronouncement, but it made me finally stop blaming myself. This realization helped me release guilt. I still have some of the old habits of reactivity of my own, and issues of low self-esteem to deal with, but I'm committed to that work. We all have things to work on in life.

I thank my healer for helping me find some peace. I hope my son will be able to increasingly find peace as well. He has deep roots connecting him to people who love him. I am one of those people.

I don't feel so hopeless anymore. I've learned that we often hear things differently. We may feel attacked or judged because of our own low self-esteem, but if we give ourselves 90 seconds to honor these feelings it is transformative. We have the power to consciously choose love. We can choose joy. We can choose passion. When we don't react to the negative feeling, when we don't hang onto the feeling, we have power to move through and process it.

I hope Jean-Paul finds a healing path. He is such an amazing person. He is beloved by so many, including his proud mama.

In my mind's eye, I see me holding Jean-Paul in one of our heart-to-heart hugs. I love him so much. As we stand together, all the anger, guilt, blame, fear, sorrow, and pain is received by our Mother Earth. We stand until there is nothing left but our embrace, our love.

Brenda Bergeron

Love Letter To The One Who Lost Hope

Maybe you're in the crevices of a life you knew but now, is no more.

Maybe you thought there were invisible promises from God or the Universe that life would stay at least familiar.

Whatever you face, maybe hope fell out of your pocket after breakfast.

Or it shattered along with a life,
and now grief is taking over in ways you can't stop.

You've tried.

Hope leaves guideposts along the way, but most don't notice because Hope never points to the way out,
only the way through:

"Here is my friend Grief. Take a walk with her for a bit."

"You are loved even though you can't feel it,
trust Grief to lead you to me."

"I know it's dark... but you are accompanied in the invisible world. You're almost back to me."

Personally signed, "Hope"

What we really want is the skeleton key to *Find Hope in 10 Easy Steps*. We want quick answers on how to make grief stop.

It doesn't work that way, love.

Here are the instructions you may be missing:

Meet Grief at the doorway - walk straight ahead.

Left turn at the tears and anger, don't be afraid of the extra dark.

Keep tears flowing as you walk.

Right turn into the first open path with a bit of light. You'll know it by the exhaustion and gray sadness that flickers at the end of the hallway.

Follow to the door leading outside.

Sit under the big Oak of Love and count the leaves as they fall, naming each one as you wish.

When you're ready, find something to eat - maybe the bowl of cereal you forgot this morning, or last night's dinner wrapped in the fridge.

Go rest.

Or scream.

Or take a long walk, and return to the tree (any tree, they all know you and are waiting for your return).

Look down at your feet.

Every step you've made has a tiny sparkle of hope. You may not feel it or see it, but it's there.

Every day you move with Grief, you are witnessed by the starry sky.

You are met by the stones or mountains or streams.

Or maybe a child's eye caught yours and they smiled.

Or, at 2 a.m., you witnessed yourself when your body refused sleep again. This time you "heard" a message: all this would make sense later.

For once you believed it.

At 2:15 a.m. you made your heart a pinky promise to hang on, even though you just wanted to awaken back to a world you once knew, now extinct.

Every step.

Every minute,

asks your courage to believe and trust that you are carving a new path for yourself.

On this self-guided path, look for the signs Grief offers, because they also point to Love.

Grief and Love walk the road of Hope....which you are on.

Love's steps and Grief's outpourings create the pebble, stone and concrete pavement of highways and backwoods shortcuts to Hope.

Keep stepping.

Remember you are loved, and as you step, Hope will meet you on the path, in the path, and with the path.

You won't miss her.

Pinky promise.

Vikki Spencer

"The secret is not to give up hope. It's very hard not to because if you're really doing something worthwhile I think you will be pushed to the brink of hopelessness before you come through the other side."

George Lucas

There's More

It's never one thing that brings us to the point of giving up. It's a million little things. Sometimes, when it becomes a million and one - it's just too much!

I want to explain some of the million little things that almost broke me. If I don't, I fear, dear reader, that you will judge me harshly. I hope if you understand my backstory, it will help you understand my choices.

I met my 'Knight' at a bustling party. I found myself sitting across from him and was immediately intrigued. He was handsome and engaging. We seemed to have a lot in common. I enjoyed him and was thrilled that he enjoyed me! He made me laugh. Before I left, of course I gave him my number. The next day he called.

Our relationship developed in warp-speed time. He hated that I was living in my parent's basement as he felt it wasn't safe. If there was a fire, I wouldn't be able to get out. I saw his concern as evidence that he cared. He became my shining 'Knight' on a white horse who was intent on 'saving' me.

Within a short time, he asked me to move in with him. In less than six months we were married. Even though it all happened incredibly fast, it felt perfect. We lived in a cute little house; had a perfect dog; traveled together; and had a busy social life with his friends. While he encouraged me to go out with my own friends, he never did anything with my friends. I overlooked that 'small' detail because it was all…perfect! At least that's what I saw at the time. There are a lot of things I see now that I didn't notice at the time. It's taken years for me to realize how one-sided the relationship was. I was blinded by what I wanted to believe.

I had never gone to college because my mother had convinced me it was too expensive and difficult for me. My Knight encouraged me to take a class. I loved it! He encouraged me to quit my job and attend full time. I decided to go for it. Why not? I had never been without a job, so I was a bit nervous. My Knight, with his shining shield of wonderfulness to the rescue, assured me that it would not be a problem. I quit my job and signed up for classes.

I loved it. I loved everything about college, the environment, and the people I connected with. It created a sense of belonging, I now had college friends. Growing up, I had never had roots because we moved frequently. I attended a different school every year, so I had never had long-term friendships. The idea of permanence and history with close friends was enticing.

My last semester of college, I went back to work. I got an exciting job offer, which the Knight encouraged me to take. The pay wasn't great, however in true Knight fashion, he said the money didn't matter. We didn't need the money. I accepted the job, and it turned out to be my favorite job of all time.

Then, a few months later, a call changed everything. I initially thought he was calling to see how my day was going. That was not the case.

Me: "Hey, how are things?"
Knight: "I want a divorce."
Me: "What the hell? You want a divorce?"
Knight: "Yes. I do not want to be married anymore."
Me: "Just like that? We aren't going to talk about it?"
Knight: "We just did."

And he hung up.

My head and the room started spinning. I had to hold on to the kitchen counter to steady myself so I didn't fall off the world. It felt as though my entire life went into a spiral. We had never talked about him being unhappy. There had been no discussion about separating. No hint that he was considering divorce. I couldn't wrap my head around what had just happened. He acted like it was no big deal. He decided, and it was so. It was years later that I realized that he had always been the one in the relationship who did the deciding. His friends; his timing; and his family. My side never mattered. I hadn't noticed that I had become cocooned in a world of his making.

Hours later he came home, sat in the chair, and read the paper. "Are we going to talk about this?" I asked.

He peeked over the paper and said, "We did. I have decided. Tomorrow I'll call my lawyer." Then, he resumed reading the paper as if nothing remarkable was happening.

I went into the bedroom, pacing back and forth like a raging bull. I felt I might explode - like there wasn't enough room inside me for all the fury. I picked something up and threw it. It crashed into the mirror, which broke into pieces. It wasn't enough to release the enormity of the rage flooding through my veins. I lost it! I just started throwing everything I could put my hands on. I screamed and punched whatever was within my reach. At no point did he come to check to see if I was okay. When I stormed out of the bedroom, he was still calmly reading the paper. I stood in front of him and yelled, "What the f#ck! Do you not care what this is doing to me?" He told me that he would make things as fair as he could, and that I would be okay. Then he left.

I was consumed with fear. I had just accepted a new job that did not pay enough for me to live alone. Why had he encouraged me to take this job if he knew he didn't want to stay married? How would I afford to live? I loved this cute little dream house and my dream life. I didn't want to move back with my parents. I didn't think I could do this. Nothing about this felt like I was going to be okay. I felt overwhelmed and hopeless. I got a glass of wine and gulped it down too quickly. It felt nice. I poured another. Then another. I thought if I drank enough, I wouldn't feel so horrible; so heartbroken; so hopeless. The first bottle went down fast, so I got another. This time I didn't bother with a glass. I sat cross-legged in the chair with my bottle and my dark thoughts.

I used to think that people who attempted suicide were selfish. How could they do that to the people they left behind? I don't anymore. I thought of my brother, who is my best friend. I hated that I was going to disappoint him and cause him pain. However, my own pain, along with the belief that I could not make it through this horrible time, was stronger than my guilt. I convinced myself he would understand. I stumbled to the bathroom, my gait unsteady, having consumed almost two bottles of wine in record time. I knew we had some pain pills in the medicine cabinet. I took them to my chair. I just wanted to end things quickly and painlessly. I washed several of the pills down with some wine. Then more. Pills - wine - repeat. I wasn't sure how much it would take to drift off into an eternal sleep, so I took them all.

I expected to simply pass out. That is not at all what happened. My chest started to hurt, and I started to have trouble breathing. I couldn't understand why I felt like an elephant was sitting on top of me. I started to panic, so I called the Knight. I'm not sure what I said because I could barely talk, but he came home. At this point, I was lying on the floor, in and out of consciousness. I have a vague memory of him talking to someone on the phone. Later I learned it was poison control. It's mind-blowing to me that he was trying to determine whether he needed to call 911. He seemed more concerned about how it might look to the neighbors than that I might be dying. The next memory I have is lying in the back of an ambulance throwing up in a bag. They were trying to determine how much wine I had consumed, and how many pills I had taken.

The next memory after that was of a strange man standing by my hospital bed welcoming me back. He smiled, took my hand, and assured me that everything was going to be alright. Knight peeked in and said now that I was awake, he was going home, and he left me alone in the hospital. The doctor told me I had to stay in the hospital a while for observation. I knew what that meant. "No! No! I don't need to stay here!" I knew I was heading to the psych ward. He just smiled again and told me it would be okay. At this point my life felt like it was no longer mine.

While in the hospital I was told where to go and when. Every action was dictated and monitored. I was told I had no choice. Overnight I went from hope, to hopeless, choices, to no choice. After a few days I was required to go to group meetings, and I was assigned a therapist. During those private sessions, the Knight was always present. I insisted that he was the reason I had tried to take my life. I placed the blame squarely on him. The therapist insisted it wasn't Knight's fault. He hadn't forced me to drink or take the pills. You, I was told, decided that. That had been my choice. I sat in the therapist's office next to Knight and heard myself repeating, "He did this," and "what about…?"

Why the hell did they not get it? Why was the therapist on his side? He's the f#cker that called me to say he didn't want to be married anymore. I was blindsided. I struggled to understand and process what had happened. Had I been so clueless that I had missed all the signs? I didn't think so. There had been no signs. I wanted to scream, "Stop saying it is not his fault! It's 100% his fault. He did this!" Still, it was all confusing. I kept vacillating between believing he did this to me, and that it was my own fault. It was hard not to blame him since his pronouncement had started the whole spiral! Part of me also felt it was no one's fault but my own. After all, we are all in charge of our own feelings - right?

The possibility that I had done this to myself made me feel even worse. I hadn't been taught the skills I needed to process the emotional grenades that life throws our way. I resisted taking responsibility for my attempted suicide, until one day I realized I might not get out of the hospital if I didn't acquiesce. I started to figure out how to play the game. If I just said what they wanted to hear, then I might get out of there sooner. I didn't really think I belonged there. Yes, I had messed up, however, I wasn't like the others who were in there! Or was I?

After a while I was allowed to go outside. It was a small enclosure, but it was still outside! I remember closing my eyes and sucking in the fresh night air. It felt so good! I walked to the fence and looked through the slats at the world beyond. I needed to see that. There was still a world out there, beyond these white cinder block walls. It gave me a spark of hope. I continued to tell them what they wanted to hear so I could go home.

A few weeks later they released me. Ironically, they made Knight in charge of my medication. The man who I still believed was the reason I was there. Every day he put a pill on the table before he left for the day. He didn't seem concerned about whether I took it or not. I followed the rules and took them like a good girl. I was required to go to therapy as part of the conditions for my release. It felt like a waste of my time. I continued to play the game, said what they wanted to hear and volunteered little. I must have played the game well, because soon I didn't have to go anymore. Game well played. Match set and point. I won.

The Knight and I lived in the same house for a while, until I found another place an hour away from my job. He helped with the initial deposit and financial outlay. After another year I moved closer to work and purchased a small condo. It was all mine! For the first time in my life, I owned my own home. Though when we divorced Knight refused to pay me alimony, for years he did send me money and gift cards. I think he did it until he felt I was "okay." I always thought of it as guilt money. Like he was making it all ok because he was "helping." After I was released from the hospital, everyone around me acted like nothing had happened. I, too, acted like nothing had happened. I never talked about it.

Several years ago, I finally opened up about what happened with a person who eventually became a fabulous mentor and life coach to me. He had a knack for saying things in a way that resonated for me. As I was telling him the story, I repeatedly said that Knight had never given me a reason he had done what he did, except that he simply didn't want to be married anymore. He boiled it down in the simplest way. "He gave you a reason. He didn't want to be married. It might not be a good reason, or one that you like, however it is a reason."

Those words were like a deep, cleansing breath! The Knight might have had a lame reason…it was his reason. I don't have to like it, understand it, or agree with it; I did, however, have the choice whether I would hold on to my anger and grief, or release it and move forward. I chose to let go and move forward.

Now, many years later I do have a whole new life. Only a few people know what happened because I still don't talk about it. I do think about it, often. I learned a great deal about myself during my time of healing from my pain and grief. I've been to the edge, and I've taken one more step. I know I'm lucky, I've been given another chance. I know I am capable of being on the edge, and rather than taking the step off, I take a breath, I pause. Because of that, even during dark times when I feel a sense of hopelessness, I never think about suicide. There are times when I wish I could just sleep it off, to wake up to find the problem has disappeared.

I also recognize that my experience has brought me to where I am today. I have two college degrees; I had the opportunity to work an amazing job for thirteen years and was able to buy my own condo.

Those too have their roots in what happened.

I wish I could tell you that it is a 'perfect ending,' but that doesn't tend to be real life. I know that healing is a process, especially when it is from a lifetime of pain. I also know that I am not alone in that struggle. We all have our stories, our struggles, short or long chapters that we wish we could have skipped. We all have pain from which we need to heal. There are times I still feel lost, lonely, and like I'm not part of something. The child in me still sometimes craves parental love and guidance. At times it still feels like I'm going through life just existing. Like life is happening all around me, and I'm sitting on the sidelines watching. Sometimes, I also think, nobody would notice if I disappeared. Then I remind myself that my brother would notice. And now I've remarried, and my loving husband would.

Who knows what's next? I can only hope each chapter is better than the last. I also know, even if the worst happens, I have successfully come back from the edge, and I never have to go there again.

There is more waiting for me; more opportunity; more learning; more growth; and probably more pain too. That's okay, because without the experience of pain, we do not know how wonderful joy, happiness and love really feels.

It is what I hold on to - there is more. There is hope.

Kathy Rae

A Legacy of Grace

Beth had a ticking bomb growing in her brain - an arteriovenous malformation (AVM).

An AVM is an abnormal, tangled, and irregular connection of blood vessels. Beth's was extremely large, involving almost an entire hemisphere of her brain. An AVM disrupts blood flow and the ability for oxygen to normally circulate. That negatively affects all vital organs, including the heart, lungs, and brain. Additionally, because the walls of the blood vessels are thinner and weaker with AVMs, it often results in an aneurysm, or bulge, in the wall of the blood vessels. An aneurysm is at risk of rupturing, which can cause bleeding into the brain and spinal cord. That can result in brain damage and neurological deficits, or even death.

The cause of an AVM isn't clear. They are sometimes, but not always, hereditary. Regardless of the underlying cause, they are much like a buried landmine waiting to explode!

Beth was diagnosed in 1984, after experiencing a seizure while driving. Luckily, nobody was seriously injured, however it was life-changing for her. She had been experiencing seizures for years, but only while sleeping. She wasn't concerned at the time because they only ever happened at night. She assumed they were because of an airplane crash she had been in as a child. The accident was the first time a seizure had ever intruded into her waking hours.

After brain scans revealed the AVM, the doctor told her that in 5 years she would either be dead or completely incapacitated. When Beth shared the doctor's diagnosis and prognosis with me, she used the word, "vegetable." The prospect was overwhelming, to say the least! Her primary concern was how it would affect her ability to be a good mother to her small children. She wanted to stay alive for them. When her husband talks about that time, he remembers, "Everything just turned gray! Eventually we emerged, but it was that way for a good long time."

Over the years that I knew Beth, she experienced three major brain bleeds, or hemorrhages, until a fourth one finally took her life in November of 2020. As the years went by, she experienced several obtrusive symptoms from the AVM, including severe headaches, grand mal seizures, nausea, and fatigue. She sought treatment from both western and eastern medicine, including radiation; medication; chiropractic care; acupuncture; herbal remedies; cranial sacral; and more. In the final analysis none of it was curative.

And yet, through it all, Beth was a patient and attentive mother. She was a loving wife. She was thoughtful and kind in her friendships. She embraced life with a new and acute awareness of its profound fragility!

As her illness progressed, Beth's body began to be wrecked with damage from the bleeds, seizures, and medical procedures. She began to experience severe neuropathy pain, muscle weakness and dysfunction, and unrelenting insomnia. She eventually began to experience a progressive loss of neurological function that affected her mobility and functionality. She lost a significant amount of the use of her left arm and leg. Her coordination began to suffer. Her gait became labored.

What is so remarkable is how she chose to 'BE' in the midst of it all. She chose to live life for as long as she was alive, and that still moves me to the deepest part of my being!

Immediately following Beth's diagnosis, she was still able, for the most part, to function normally. The one thing she couldn't do was drive. The risk of having another seizure while driving was too high. Not being able to drive may sound trivial, but I now have a greater appreciation for the enormous impact it has! I personally have been unable to drive for the last three years due to visual impairment. It shrinks your world substantially. It makes you dependent.

If you have been fiercely independent your whole life, as Beth certainly was, that is a harsh blow! Suddenly she had to work around everyone else's schedule, which was difficult at times. Her husband, Rand, had a job that required frequent travel and time away from home. They had two small children and a busy household to run. They would often host people, as was sometimes required due to Rand's job.

Not being able to drive added another layer to an already busy and complicated schedule. But she made things work. Sometimes it required forethought and planning because she needed transportation or assistance. Sometimes Rand had to adjust his schedule to ensure she had what she needed. It became increasingly about teamwork and relationships, an area in which she excelled!

I learned a great deal about patience and the virtue of graceful acceptance from Beth. As time passed, and her disabilities became more substantial, her ability to do it all began to diminish. And, though the people who loved her were supportive and present, there were times when schedules did not perfectly align. When this happened, she sometimes had to wait for - or sometimes forgo - what she used to so easily do for herself. This could be frustrating. But instead of growing bitter, she chose instead to practice letting go and accepting things as less than perfect, or at least different than how she wanted and preferred it to be.

She also valued herself enough to make her needs known, and to ask for help. When people become more dependent on others, they sometimes begin to feel like a burden. But she knew her worth. She seemed able to clearly make her needs and preferences known. She was always grateful for the help she received, but I don't remember ever seeing her apologetic or acting as if she wasn't worth other people's time and energy. That example, for me, was a powerful reminder that our value is inherent, and not based on anything we can or cannot do.

Beth did not make a habit of complaining about her lot. She would honestly communicate about how she was feeling and the struggles she faced, but she didn't make it a constant topic of conversation. She didn't allow herself to become so consumed by her own suffering that she lost sight of other things and the needs of other people.

She was, however, ready for death long before she died. She longed for that release from her suffering. Though it wasn't information she volunteered, she was honest about it when asked. But she also strongly believed that until she died, she had work to do! She spent hours every day reading books that nourished and uplifted her spirit, so that she had the spiritual and emotional resources to do that work! This was a daily practice, especially after she became confined to bed. She read the Bible and other books about love, faith, joy, and hope. She personified the words in these books.

I remember being struck by her capacity to think of others amid her own pain and suffering. She prayed for others - often, especially at night. People who have never experienced insomnia often don't realize what a lonely and isolating experience it can be. Since she was unable to sleep, she decided to dedicate that time in the service of prayer. This kept her from getting caught up in the spin of sleepless despair. She ended up connecting several friends, and even complete strangers, who were also experiencing ongoing and profound insomnia. This evolved into a regular nighttime prayer vigil that she called 'The Starlight Prayer Ministry.' It provided many with a sense of purpose and strength, instead of the isolation and frustration they had previously experienced.

In addition to her prayer ministry, she often called to check in with people who were struggling or ill. She did so, even when she, herself, could barely get out of bed. Beth always had a stack of greeting cards nearby so that she could send people notes of encouragement. I received many cards of appreciation, love, and encouragement over the years - even during the years when she struggled to write, walk, sleep, and perform basic everyday tasks. The cards kept coming - until she died.

People say that a person continues to live on in the hearts and minds of those they loved. That is true of Beth! She lives in my heart and in the hearts of her family, and all of those who were touched by her loving kindness. I have been able to walk through some of the darkest times in my life because of her example of how to do so with some measure of grace. She demonstrated that, even in our most trying, difficult moments, we can refuse to become utterly consumed by our own experience. We can choose to remember that others may also be suffering, and that we can be a source of comfort and encouragement for them.

I am convinced that one of the primary reasons Beth was able to walk such a difficult life path with so much grace is because of the time she spent uplifting and providing the light of encouragement to others. In doing so, she unexpectedly lit her own path with grace and strength.

Beth Holm (as told by her best friend, Diane Gross.)

"The bravest thing I ever did was continuing my life when I wanted to die."

Juliette Lewis, The Grace Year

Audacious Hope

To genuinely appreciate a person's heroic journey through darkness, we must first understand what they lost. An accident resulting in substantial and permanent damage to a knee, for example, may be a much harder blow for a world-class Olympian than for the average person because they would suffer the loss of their career and life-long dream. Sometimes the measure of pain and grief can be best understood when calculated in terms of the losses experienced.

After reading the previous story in this book, *A Legacy of Grace*, I felt inspired to share some of my own memories of Beth that highlight her courage in the face of devastating loss.

Beth and I were married for 46 years before she passed away in 2020. We first met in college. One of the first things I learned about her was that she was formidable. She demonstrated exceptional physical strength and prowess, as well as mental fortitude. She was, by any standard, an incredibly powerful athlete.

One of the areas in which Beth's athleticism manifested was with horses. She loved them - especially the more fiery and spirited ones. She wasn't interested in riding the more tame, docile horses. That was more my style. I tended to choose the old army war horses that were easy to ride, and bomb-proof. She was drawn to the meanest, toughest, and most challenging horses in the stable. One horse she loved to ride was, ironically, named Candy - because she was anything but sweet. Just catching her would often require a lot of time and perseverance. It wasn't unusual for Beth to spend as much as an hour catching Candy and fit her with a bridle and halter. Of course, Beth, badass that she was, would ride bareback. I sometimes wondered if she was drawn to Candy and other feisty horses because their fire and spirit resonated with her own.

A few months after Beth and I started dating, my parents came to campus to visit. We took them to see the horse ranch. We noticed a colt who had gotten separated from its mother and was starting to panic. Beth immediately jumped into action. She was able to corral it in a 15x15 enclosure. She attempted repeatedly to catch it, but it did not want to be caught. It was going ballistic. I remember watching the scene unfold before me and thinking, "How do you catch a panicked, rambunctious colt that doesn't want to be caught?" Suddenly I noticed Beth was no longer standing upright, but was horizontal, shooting like a fast missile toward the colt. I was shocked - and impressed. I also didn't want to appear to be a timid wimp, so I jumped off the fence and joined the fray. Beth tackled it from behind its shoulders and threw it to the ground. Then, all hell broke loose. The colt began to flail its legs in all directions. Though it was a colt, it still weighed substantially more than either of us. I grabbed its back legs, and Beth grabbed its front legs, and we dragged the struggling, terrified colt back to its mom. I will never forget the astonished look on my parents' faces.

My dad leaned over and quietly asked me, "Son, is she always like this? Is this her normal self?" As I looked over at Beth and pondered my dad's question, a sense of awe settled over me and I replied, "Yeah, dad. I think so."

That was Beth - fearless.

Then, in 1984 she had a severe seizure while driving with our two small children. The car veered across two lanes of traffic, plowed through a fence, barreled unscathed between two large trees, and came to a stop in the middle of a field. As providence would have it, a police officer had been right behind their car. He followed them, fully expecting to find a drunk driver behind the wheel. What he found instead was Beth still in the throes of a massive seizure.

Since this was before the advent of cell phones, I didn't know what happened for many hours. I had a message waiting for me on the house phone from the police officer who had been at the scene of Beth's accident. In an act of incredible kindness, he had spent all day with her. The hospital ordered a CAT scan. It was the day before Mother's Day. The doctor suggested that we wait to hear the results until after Mother's Day. We couldn't. The stress of waiting was overwhelming. That day we learned Beth had an Arteriovenous Malformation (AVM). Over the next few weeks and months, we were told that the prognosis for an AVM was a long, slow, and horrible death.

Our nice, warm, and beautiful life suddenly turned to gray ashes. All the joy was sucked out of us. Each doctor we spoke with offered a dim view of life if she lived. They told us she might be better off if she died sooner rather than later. They offered little hope for anything other than a miserable life.

What followed was the worst year of our lives. We were living in the gray. Life became something to just get through. Then, Beth made a pivotal and courageous decision that changed everything. She decided she was going to live with the AVM rather than die with it.

After a while we were referred by her neurologist to one of the top neurosurgeons in the world. He offered hope. It felt like he was holding out water as we were languishing from thirst in a desert.

There was a new and promising procedure called Proton Beam Therapy. The technology was still in its infancy and had never been used before for such a large area as the AVM in Beth's brain, but they thought it might improve her prognosis and outcome. Sadly, it did not. It made it worse. Immediately she went from one seizure a year to one per month. It was a disheartening turn of events.

None of the medical interventions Beth tried over the years helped. Her illness slowly, but irrevocably, stole her physical strength and abilities. But her courageous spirit remained intact. Her strength of character and internal fortitude enabled her to find hope within herself. I believe it is that audacious hope that enabled her to live 36 years with her AVM. Even with her losses, she lived a life that was filled with joy, laughter, friends, and family.

The way she lived taught me that when all hope is gone, you must create hope. The way she lived with her disability reminds me of the way she approached the panicked colt when it was separated from its mother. She knew that sometimes you must tackle an out of control, untamable situation full on. You go in swinging and see what you can accomplish. You grab hold and, if possible, throw it to the ground. Win or lose - you try. Whatever your losses - you do what you can. You don't just sit on the fence and observe, hoping for the best. You give it your best. You give hope your best.

Beth showed tremendous courage in the face of great loss. She had the audacity to manufacture and create hope along the way, even when it seemed that all hope was gone.

She had audacious hope.

Rand Holm

"Your hope is the most beautiful and the saddest in the world."

Naomi Benaron

Let Hope Find You

At eight years old, I got separated from my mom at an amusement park gift shop. She always told me to go to the last place I saw her. She would meet me there. As I look back, I find it interesting that her instructions weren't to stay where I was, but to go to the place we last saw each other.

I couldn't find her at the rock candy rack where we looked at the flavors. So I told a clerk I was lost. She called security, and paged my mom.

I was in tears, not knowing where to go or what to do next. I was scared I might be left behind!

Thankfully, my mom heard the page and came to the register where I was standing.

"Where were you?" I cried.

"I went to go find you," she said. "I didn't see you in the store, so I went back to the line of the last ride you went on to see if you were there. But, I'm here now."

Through the years, I would learn to use this direction to locate myself, and Hope.

My mom's instruction to go to the last place translated through the years to go where I last knew Hope. This has seemed like the only strategy that has helped me re-center amidst devastating losses in my life.

I knew Hope was at a mountain hiking trail near the waterfall - and she met me there.

I knew Hope was in the evening candle I used to light for dinner - and there she was.

I knew Hope was always in a sun ray that came through the window, and as I positioned myself, there she was.

I knew Hope was at a favorite coffee shop as I wrote in my journal, and sure enough, she was there with her cappuccino, waiting for me.

In time, I've learned of Hope's resilience and impossibility to lose.

I'm not afraid because I've already lost her three times today.

Each time when I came to an endpoint, I sat still and let her find me.

She knows where I am.

Vikki Spencer

"When you get tired learn to rest, not quit."

Banksy

The Game of Life

In December of 2014, my twenty-year-old son, Jordan, started to complain of severe back pain. He was an avid gamer, so we initially assumed the pain was due to how much time he spent sitting on the floor of the basement playing. Virtually all his free time, when he wasn't working or attending college classes, was spent gaming. But when his symptoms persisted for more than a week, he went to see the doctor.

The doctor recommended an MRI, which Jordan was able to get done quickly. The following day he went alone to get the results. I couldn't imagine it was going to be anything serious, so I stayed at work. It turned out that his symptoms were not due to his excessive gaming. They found a tumor on his cervical spine, which had caused a fracture in his vertebrae as it had grown. No wonder he was in so much pain! The doctor suggested we contact an oncologist as soon as possible for more testing. It was the beginning of an exceptionally long and stressful journey.

We made an appointment with an oncologist at the University of Maryland Medical Center (UMMC) in Baltimore. They were able to see him immediately. The doctor suggested that, since Jordan was young, he should be admitted to the Pediatric Oncology Department. This would allow for a more aggressive approach to treatment, as well as ensure he could be monitored for a 10-year follow-up period.

The week flew by. There were phone calls with UMMC, as well as other doctors for consultation. We also tried to keep family and friends updated. Everyone was, of course, concerned. On Thursday, just three days after the initial diagnosis, Jordan was admitted to the Pediatric Hematology and Oncology unit. He was scheduled for surgery the following day.

The plan was multi-faceted: to remove the tumor; repair the fractured vertebrae; determine the type of cancer; and begin chemotherapy. I decided to take a leave of absence from my work as a freelance Sign Language Interpreter. I knew Jordan had a long road ahead of him, and I wanted to be there as much as possible to support him.

During his surgery, family members and friends came to support me and my husband, Stewart. Even our Rabbi came. But I couldn't handle conversations or interacting with anyone. I just waved people away when they came to check on me. I curled up in a fetal position with a pillow and blanket in the hospital surgical waiting area and prayed. I couldn't help worrying about all that could go wrong. I was so scared. My mind was racing with a million doubts and questions:

Had we explored all viable options? Should we have gotten a second opinion?

How long would the recovery take? Would there be any long-term effects for Jordan?

What if he ended up paralyzed? How would our twelve-year-old daughter, Samantha, feel about her parents spending so much time with her brother?

Jordan's surgeon came highly recommended. That afforded some measure of comfort, but it was still terrifying. The surgery took several hours but felt like a lifetime. He ended up removing what he could and built a titanium cage around the fractured vertebrae in his spine. When the surgery was completed, he stated he suspected it was 'a good kind of cancer,' because of how it had melted like butter on his scalpel. It would, however, be a few days until we had biopsy results to confirm what kind of cancer had invaded my son's body. It turned out to be Diffuse Large B-Cell Lymphoma. This is an aggressive and fast-growing cancer. So, time tends to be of the essence.

Chemotherapy could not begin until Jordan had healed some from the surgery. He had to remain hospitalized for a total of twenty-six days. When ready, Jordan received chemo every three weeks for a total of six months. When it was time for his next round he was admitted to the pediatric floor of the hospital. I stayed with him overnight as much as possible. My husband came to visit after work and on weekends whenever possible and did his best to take care of Samantha.

On the pediatric floor of the hospital there were many little children, their parents by their bedside. The children were hooked up to machines in a scary hospital room instead of at home with their families; their toys; their books; and their belongings; and their favorite home-cooked food. Watching my own son in pain, as well as the suffering of the other children and parents, was excruciating and overwhelming. I tried to stay positive about Jordan's situation, but it was challenging.

It was all beyond exhausting. There were days when I didn't have the time or energy to shower or eat more than a bite of food. I slept in an uncomfortable hospital chair in Jordan's room. I woke to every vitals check and administering of medication. I was attuned to every time Jordan moved or moaned in pain. I lived on cafeteria food and was grateful that it was quite good. They regularly made Mac and cheese, which was Jordan's favorite food on earth. I purchased some for him whenever he was up to eating. I later learned that a high protein diet is often recommended to help with post-surgical healing. I was livid that the surgeon never said a word to us about this. Jordan's diet since his surgery had consisted mostly of Mac and cheese in every imaginable form. While we were glad to see him eating, and junk food was at the top of his preferred list of foods, it still would have been good to know that some higher protein foods might have been beneficial.

I was comfortable in medical settings due to my work, as I often interpreted in a medical setting. That exposure was helpful in this situation. I asked the doctors a lot of questions and took copious notes. Stewart was the researcher. He would read up on the treatment plans and medications, then report back with his findings, along with more questions for the doctors.

Four weeks post-surgery, Jordan's surgical wound began to ooze. His surgeon wanted me to clean his wound at home. That was not going to happen. I didn't feel like I had the necessary skills for that kind of delicate procedure. So, his doctor decided to reopen Jordan's incision, clean it out and close it back up. He was four weeks post-op, and now suddenly he was facing another surgery. It felt like we were starting again at square one. It was beyond frustrating and discouraging. How was this possible? But Jordan had made a lot of progress and seemed to have a more positive outlook than he had in quite a while. There was some comfort in that fact.

So, he had the surgery to clean everything out, and the recuperation process started again.

Jordan went through a total of four rounds of chemotherapy. He had his port removed four months after his last surgery and began the first of many follow-up appointments over the years. He received two units of blood. I have been a blood donor since I was sixteen years old, and I decided to 'pay back' those two units he received - plus one more unit as a 'thank you.' It felt good to be able to do…something.

One night, during some of the most intense times, my own physician, a breast cancer survivor, called to see how things were going.

She said that at some point I would look back and be grateful, not for the cancer, but for the lessons learned from the experience. As I look back on that time, I realize she was right. I learned what was important in life. I learned who was important. I learned that with the right mindset, we can get through anything.

I'd like to share some of the thoughts, realizations, and lessons I learned during this difficult six-month journey:

o I didn't really need much to survive. I spent most of my days in Jordan's room. All I really needed was to spend time with my family. I learned the difference between need and want.

o My real friends showed up - literally. They reached out by phone and email to let me know they were there for us. My best friend drove down from Connecticut to be with me and provide support. Another friend worked at the hospital where Jordan was being treated. She came to visit during breaks and frequently before she went home. I learned who my real friends were.

o Ask and you shall receive. I don't tend to ask people for favors, but people were there for us in so many ways. For example, our bathroom sink developed a big crack in it while Jordan was in the hospital. It had to be replaced. Our neighbor came over, assessed the situation, bought a new sink, and installed it for us.

I learned the value of asking for and accepting help.

o   People will step out of their comfort zone to help. Jordan's hair started to fall out a few weeks into chemo treatments. It was falling onto his pillow and into his eyes. It was starting to drive him crazy. We invented 'tape therapy.' We used medical tape to remove loose hairs, much like how a lint brush works. Still, we couldn't get all the hair removed. When I told my hairdresser about it, even though she was not comfortable in Baltimore traffic, she had her husband drive her to the hospital so she could shave the remainder of Jordan's hair off. I learned that people were willing to sacrifice their own comfort to help.

o   No one knows what someone is going through - so just be kind. You can't look at someone and know their son has cancer. You can't know their mother just died, or they just lost their job, or are having a difficult day. We really have no idea why someone may behave rudely or be abrupt. I remember walking through Target one afternoon when my husband gave me a break from the hospital. I was depressed and upset with all that was happening. But as I walked through the store, it struck me that nobody there knew my son had cancer. They had no idea I was basically living at the hospital. No one knew he was as sick as a dog from the chemo. Nobody there knew what it felt like to hear him say, "It hurts so bad Mom." They didn't know the anguish of knowing all I could do was try to get some help from the hospital staff, because I couldn't help him myself. I realized that no one there knew what was happening in my world at that moment. It made me acutely aware that I needed to be more mindful that I too, might not know what was happening in other people's lives when I interacted with them. I learned to give people the benefit of the doubt and err on the side of kindness.

- o We can't walk someone else's path. I would have changed places with Jordan in a heartbeat. It seemed so unfair that he was sick. His cancer appeared to be related to medications he had to take for ulcerative colitis as a young teen. It was hard to watch him suffer for something that wasn't at all his fault. I learned that I couldn't walk his path for him. I could only be by his side and support him as he walked it. That's all we can ever do.

- o Prioritizing things of importance can be heartbreaking. I often wished I could have split myself in two. I wanted to be at the hospital with Jordan and I wanted to be at home with my daughter, Samantha. She wasn't seeing much of her mom. That is hard for a child. I was incredibly grateful to have a husband who was involved. We were a great team as we dealt with important things on both the hospital and home fronts. I learned that we need each other.

- o Document everything. The whole experience was overwhelming. I was exhausted and stressed. So, I kept a notebook to document Jordan's vitals, comments from doctors, and test results. This made it possible to share accurate and up-to-date information with my husband. I wrote down questions that came to mind, which happened at all hours of the day and night. Doing this freed my mind from having to keep all the information in my head. I learned to build strategies to cope.

o People's kindness mattered. I feel tremendous gratitude for the kindness that put a smile on my son's face. I remember, for example, Santa and the Baltimore Oriole mascot came to visit Jordan. Anything that could put a smile on my son's face in the midst of his pain was gold to me. A gift from Santa did that. A home-made fleece Ravens blanket did that. The Oriole Bird did that. I learned we can make a difference and bring a smile into the lives of others.

o Show appreciation for others. We put a huge bowl of candy in Jordan's room, keeping it always filled. It was there for all staff, including nurses, doctors, janitorial staff, techs, and people who transported him from place to place within the hospital. It was a simple way to show our appreciation to an overworked and often unappreciated staff. And, just maybe, Jordan got a little more attention when they came into his room to grab a sweet treat. I learned that giving and receiving are often indistinguishable.

o Look for the silver lining. Jordan had extremely high doses of medications for his cancer treatment that he had taken when he had colitis. A silver lining and unexpected outcome is that he hasn't had a colitis flare since his chemotherapy. I learned that even in misfortune there is sometimes a gift.

Jordan just had his ten-year oncology checkup. It has been a grueling long haul, but he is finally able to put it all behind him. And so too, am I. He is now living in a beach town where he works as a waiter.

He still plays too many video games! More importantly though, we've all gained some valuable experience in the Game of Life.

Robin Schwartz

Persevering to Joy

While eating a salad during lunch with my colleagues, a sharp pain sliced through the back of my right jaw. Had I broken a tooth? My tongue went to the spot. Everything was intact. The pain subsided. Another bite brought needle-like jabs to my jaw muscle. Sharp pain stung my cheek and temple, leaving a lingering ache afterward. I put my fork down and, puzzled, asked for a take-home box. I would need to see a dentist.

The dentist was mystified as I was. I had inherited a jaw that wouldn't allow my teeth to meet efficiently, and surgery to reconstruct my jaws in my teen years had temporarily corrected it. The operation had slightly injured a nerve in my lower jaw, leaving my chin and lip partially numb. A late growth spurt in high school had undone the surgeon's work, and my orthodontist tried to rework my bite with simple braces. Wires that were normally left behind in my type of procedure worked loose during the growth spurt and had to be surgically removed. Only two wires remained, deeply buried in the back of my lower jawbone on each side. A local oral surgeon removed one, but the other wire was stuck against a nerve, causing my current issue.

Chewing caused sharp and continued pain; I completely switched my diet to soft foods. Talking to anyone, including my students in my teaching job, was sometimes unbearable; I quit socializing outside of work. Sometimes the pain occurred for no apparent reason. Strong wind triggered needle jabs in my temple; I stopped my outdoor activities. This was the beginning of my traumatic odyssey of chronic pain. I was becoming a different person.

My dentist referred me to a large university hospital oral surgeon, a four-hour drive away. Over the next four years several operations were performed, utilizing the latest technology to remove the offending wire and try to repair the nerve damage. The university doctors referred me to a medical pain clinic, a chronic pain support group, and individual psychological counseling. I used all my sick leave from work to make the frequent trips for appointments, sometimes as often as twice a week. At first the surgery improved things, but the jabs and constant pain soon came roaring back.

The pain clinic physician gave me a parade of pills and infusions to see what might help. Very few medications made any difference. I was exhausted from the trials, overwhelmed by balancing appointment schedules with my job, and beyond hope that anything might cure my chronic pain. My world seemed so small – no social outings, no talking on the phone for any length of time. I wrote many letters to my friends and family, trying to feel connected in some way.

The psychologist helped me work through some of my despondent questions: How was I ever to get through this? How could I continue to work and support myself? Was the depression from my experiences or was it physiological?

I was afraid that I might have to stop teaching and seek long-term disability. I dreaded the thought. My inner esteem depended on being self-sustaining, fully employed, supporting others. I took a temporary leave of absence from my job to give my health a rest and see if I could just... heal.

I returned to work after three months, determined to make my life, my autonomy, my fierce spirit of independence, work for me in some way. My days became very methodical as I kept meticulous records, noting times, pain levels, and activities or foods that might have contributed to a flare-up.

I threw myself into my work and volunteered for tasks in which I could use sign language instead of talking. I exercised regularly to maximize my health. I continued seeing my psychological counselor, especially when I was in a slump of self-doubt with out-of-control pain. With every successful active day, I had a renewed determination. More than anything I prayed for answers, for a path forward.

Five years after the pain began, I had the opportunity to volunteer to lead backpacking trips at a summer youth camp, something that had always been dear to my heart. Motivation! I researched a backpack that wouldn't pull or aggravate the injured nerve. Planning trails, developing healthy dried food recipes that I could chew, and figuring out my gear became a delightful hobby during the school year. Leading backpacking during the summer required some talking, but I was able to ease into it. I had discovered magic for my pain: distraction in doing something I loved.

For the next five years I enjoyed my routines – social interactions with my beloved friends and Deaf community, planning exciting backpacking adventures for each summer, and continuing in my teaching job. I felt as close to my true self as I could while dealing with devastating facial pain and consequent medication. My social life expanded as I found ways to connect with people that didn't trigger my injured nerve.

Seeking answers, I attended several national conferences presenting the latest information in surgical and medical options for facial neuropathic pain and treatment. It was reassuring to learn that my own university physicians were doing all they could for me according to the latest research.

Ten years after my facial pain began, I developed severe penetrating ulcers. I was hospitalized with terrible abdominal aches and diarrhea. The all-too-familiar routine of seeing specialists, doing medical tests, and having the doctors puzzle over my condition began again. First, I was given medication to heal the ulcers.

For two more years, my abdominal symptoms continued. I became weak from the severe pain and alarming weight loss. I tried different high-caloric diets, necessarily with soft foods because of my

94

facial pain. Nothing helped. I was convinced that I was dying. I drew up my Will and told my family. As fulfilling as it had been, I mourned my life, wishing I could have traveled more, spent more time with my parents and siblings, and explored more outdoor adventures. I convinced myself that I had done everything that God had intended for me to do and that was enough. I was prepared to let my life go.

After many tests and trials, the doctors found a small benign tumor in my stomach. When they surgically removed the tumor, they found and removed adhesions in my abdominal cavity that were sometimes wrapping around my intestines, almost certainly the cause of my ongoing symptoms. I was cautiously relieved. After all, I had been through so much with my jaw pain. I wasn't fully convinced that a single operation could fix anything.

Happily, over the next two years my abdominal issues slowly resolved. I regained some weight and returned to many of my regular activities. My life began to take on a new normal. The facial pain remained, but I was managing it well with my medication.

My reprieve from certain death, as I saw it, had me reevaluating my life. Surely life was more than just working and being hyper-vigilant about my pain and my health. I couldn't fathom why I had been saddled with chronic pain, but I held onto my faith. At only forty years old, I yearned for a more fulfilling life. I wanted to do some of the things I had mourned when I thought I was dying. I also wanted to find a life companion.

Once again, my determination and self-sufficiency gave me direction. I began taking classes I liked. I attended church more regularly. I achieved my national sign language interpreting certification. I traveled to a different country, outside of my comfort zone. I joined an online dating service. I refused to allow my pain and health concerns from the past fourteen years to dictate my life.

A few months and many digital dates later, I met someone I wanted to get to know. Our mutual interests and beliefs gave us a connection before we ever met in person. A year and a half later we were married.

I couldn't have asked for a better diversion than marrying the love of my life! My husband was very patient with the albatross of my facial pain, and his patience allowed me to better compartmentalize the pain as we focused on our marriage and our lives together. Our mutual support and love for each other became my most pleasant permanent distraction, allowing me to release my former isolating self-sufficiency and therefore quit prioritizing the pain. Within two years of being married, I was able to reduce my pain medication to less than half. In another two years, I no longer required any strong pain medication.

God answered my prayers from my darkest years with more joy in the companionship of my marriage than I could ever imagine. My husband and I have shared some wonderful journeys together even as I still deal with my neuropathic pain.

Looking back, I realize that more than half my life has been spent negotiating the hierarchy of chronic pain in my daily routine. I have become a different person once again, my true self, facing the adventures of life instead of the constant obstacles of facial pain. I am profoundly grateful for this blessed fulfillment as my journey joyfully continues.

Helen Dickey

"Your hope is the most beautiful and the saddest in the world."

Naomi Benaron

Envisioning Self Advocacy

"I see something I'm concerned about. Follow me down the hall. I'd like to run some tests." I sensed the optometrist was trying to be calm. I felt mounting anxiety: My cheeks flushed, and my pulse raced. I had anticipated I would simply get a new prescription for a pair of glasses. What was going on? She ran several tests and announced I had an elevated optic nerve. I had no idea what that meant. She gave me no further information. Instead, she referred me to a specialist for further tests.

I have always been conflicted about how to address my own health challenges. My father was a general surgeon who tended to minimize any concerns about his own health. My mother tended to focus a great deal on health-related issues - including other people's. We are bombarded with overdramatized ads that advise us to, "Ask your doctor if this medication is right for you." As a result, I've sometimes slipped into a kind of fugue state regarding my own health.

Unfortunately, I had three months to wait before I could see the specialist about my optic nerve. That allowed plenty of time for me to consider every possible outcome and bounce between thoughts like, "This is nothing and I'm overreacting" and "This could be serious." Those three months were an eternity! When the day of the appointment finally arrived, the neuro ophthalmologist ran a battery of tests including a spinal tap. The resulting diagnosis was Idiopathic Intracranial Hypertension (also called Pseudo Tumor Cerebri). Idiopathic Intracranial Hypertension is a condition that happens when pressure inside the skull increases, without a known cause. The symptoms mimic those of a brain tumor, even though there is no tumor present. It can cause a variety of health concerns including vision loss. During the consultation following the diagnosis, the doctor reiterated what many have told me my whole life, "You need to lose weight." This time the doctor added, "If you don't lose weight, you could go blind." As soon as I heard those words, I was overcome with shame and fear.

I felt numb.

As I felt myself disassociating from this surreal moment, I could only hear fragments of what he explained: "Lose at least 20% of your bodyweight." "Idiopathic means we don't know the cause." "For some reason it has helped others with this diagnosis to lose weight." "This condition tends to impact women during childbearing years" "If you can't lose the weight, we can prescribe medication that might help. But the medication has side effects." My own thoughts swirled in my head. Lose weight? Sure! As easy as flying to Mars for most people.

I felt hopeless.

Of course, losing vision for anyone is huge. I imagined how I would grieve the loss of my career as an American Sign Language (ASL) interpreter and educator, and my passions for visual arts and exploring the beauty of nature. And what about my independence?

With overwhelming fear and trepidation, I dove into a weight loss program. There is nothing else quite like fear serving as motivation to make some lifestyle changes. I considered it my opportunity to do whatever I could within my control to stay healthy. Although 2 years later I had been assured my optic nerve had been restored to normal, I'll never know for sure if it was due to the significant amount of weight I lost or the fact I made it through menopause.

Six years later, I moved from Minnesota to Michigan. As I was adapting to life in a new state, I began to experience changes in my vision again. During a routine eye exam, it became evident corrective lenses were not going to be enough. At that time, the new ophthalmologist explained I might have macular degeneration. Once again, the doctor wanted to run more tests and expected me to wait 6 months. Familiar waves of fear and panic took over. This time instead of wrestling with months of sleepless nights, I shopped around for and found a new ophthalmologist who understood my urgent need for a second opinion. I was relieved to learn that I had the dry form of macular degeneration. This meant I was not likely to lose my vision. After opting to have the recommended cataract surgery, I was able to see clearly again.

Being faced with possible vision loss twice in my life was

101

traumatic for me. I am committed to remaining on a broader quest to define my own optimal health, striving to be more proactive while reducing my tendency to overreact or minimize health challenges. I've always been a dedicated advocate for others. This journey has taught me the value of being a resilient advocate for myself and to prioritize my own self-care.

Catharine Van Nostrand

A Year of Flooding

I used to frequently dream of people knocking at the door, so initially I thought the knocking was just another weird dream. But it was louder and more persistent than usual. Finally, a voice broke through, rousing me from sleep. I got up and stumbled to the door, cracking it open to find a rain-soaked woman in her pajamas.

"It's flooding!" she yelled, pointing at my lawn, but I only saw darkness.

"It's flooding!" She repeated, with more urgency. As I looked closer through the driving rain, I could see something slowly moving across my front yard.

And then she took off, down to the next house, where I imagined she must have been doing this for some time. I stepped onto my front stoop to get a better look, and it finally clicked what she was saying. Rising, quickly, was a large pool of water that was covering my front yard. And my neighbor's front yard. And the street.

My neighbor Jim was standing on his lawn, looking as confused as I felt. Stepping off my porch into ankle deep water, I slowly made my way over to him. We didn't speak at first, just looked at each other silently. The situation seemed too big for words. Eventually he motioned to his backyard, saying "come look at the river."

The Harpeth River is small and unassuming, more reminiscent of a stream than a river. It sits about forty feet down a bank from houses and has never been a concern for flooding. But at that moment it was anything but placid. It had risen forty feet and was now invading my neighbor's backyard. With the still fierce rainfall, we knew it wasn't even close to over yet.

"We need to move our cars to higher ground," Jim said softly, not looking at me. "And put your belongings up high, in case the water comes into our houses." My mind still couldn't grasp that possibility.

We stood and watched the river rise for a few minutes. Everything felt surreal and slowed down, as if in a dream. Eventually, I stirred, gave him a weak smile, and headed home in a daze. Once there, I took his advice and moved my car to higher ground. That decision ended up saving it from being ruined.

Walking back from my car, the water was now above my knees. By the time I got back to my house the water was only inches away from the entrance. That snapped me out of my daze. I started to move quickly and with purpose, stuffing things into my backpack that mattered to me the most, including my camera, phone, and some clothing.

I was trying to move vulnerable things to a safer place when there was a loud knock at the door. Two firemen were going door to door. "We're evacuating everyone - NOW!" It was then I noticed the water pouring into my house. Anything I hadn't had time to save was now fair game. I paused on the way out, casting one long look at the home filled with so many memories and feelings. I had bought this house with my soon to be ex-husband, and was just starting to make it feel like my own. I had dreams for this house, and it felt like those dreams were getting washed away with the river. With a deep sense of foreboding, I stepped into waist high water and was brought to higher ground.

The next day the flood waters had receded enough so that I could safely check on my home. I walked slowly down a very different looking street, finding the state of my house to be a total shock. The windows were blown out; the shutters sideways; someone else's shed was in my driveway; and a boat was freakishly wedged in one of my trees. A water line ran just below the roof of the house, marking how high the flood waters had risen.

The stench of stagnant river water clung to every surface. The inside of my house was painted with mud, and it looked like a tornado had gone through it. My floorboards were curling up; my refrigerator was on its side; and my drywall was so soft that I could push my hand through it. Nothing seemed to have survived the destruction.

I spent the next week emptying the contents of my house onto the lawn. I needed to assess what could be saved, and to attempt to minimize the growth of mold. Friends and family came from all over to help. Stacking everything I owned onto the front lawn, I quickly realized that almost nothing could be salvaged. Down the street every lawn looked the same- an endless muddy graveyard of the lives we had just been living.

As I waded through the debris, the shock began to be overtaken by profound fatigue. The flood waters had destroyed not only the 'things' in my life but had also swept away all that was familiar and comfortable. I had to stay with friends. I didn't know if FEMA would give me money to help. My phone continually buzzed from calls and texts, and I could barely focus at work.

I began to have frequent emotional breakdowns. But I also didn't have the luxury of stopping to process all that had happened. There were things I had to do. I had to clean the house. I had to remove all the drywall and insulation before the mold took over. I was running on fumes and severely traumatized - I just wasn't aware of it yet. So, I pushed on, trying not to think of the long road ahead.

Three months later I was still trying to find a sense of normalcy. I had a new apartment, and generous donations had replaced most of the items I had lost. I was back to work full time, and trying to rebuild my house. FEMA came through with some money, and I found a contractor who thought he could rebuild my home within budget. The days felt long, and I was still incredibly exhausted, but felt I was managing fairly well. I had always been a 'strong person,' someone who was able to keep going during tough times. So, I just kept going…

I was driving back to my apartment one rainy day when I noticed a small stream of water running across the road. I hadn't been thinking about the flood, but the sight of it shook loose all the pent-up emotions and trauma.

I began to shake so badly I had to pull off the road. I sat in my car, heart racing, and sobbed in a way I hadn't since the flood. It took a long time before I was calm enough to drive home. That was the moment I knew I was not okay, and that maybe I wasn't handling things so well after all.

Six months after the flood I found myself despondent. Sunlight streamed through the curtains onto my bed, where I had been lying for hours. I had been like this for weeks, struggling unsuccessfully to find the will to get up.

I was living in a new place with a new boyfriend, Dave. I felt emotionally broken, and he had been there for me to lean on. There were also some red flags - which I carefully ignored. Like his increasing jealousy, or how I had started to notice the little ways he was controlling. I found myself withdrawing from friends and activities. It just seemed easier to keep him happy than to argue about who I was with in my spare time.

Life seemed to be collapsing around me. I felt trapped and couldn't see a way out of despair. Sometimes I wondered if life was even worth living, or if it might be easier for everyone if I just wasn't around. Sometimes I didn't think I had it in me to keep going.

Outside the sun was setting, and I was still in bed. Dave came home and laid next to me, his hand finding mine in the dying light. I tried not to cringe when we touched. Instead, I turned away and stared into the darkness, the emptiness of the room swallowing us both.

Eight months after the flood, I found myself sitting in a therapist's office. We started doing some work around my PTSD, tackling the big issues: loss of home, loss of a safety net, loss of sense of self, and the chaos within because of it all. Two months into the sessions we were discussing an incident that happened with Dave. I had done something he didn't like, and he had responded by screaming at me and calling me ugly names. After the argument I collapsed in the shower, sobbing, my body shaking from fear. For the first time it had occurred to me that I might not be safe.

He could be loving and kind one moment, then become extremely jealous, accusative, and verbally abusive. The next day would come apologies, flowers, excuses, and loving words. I leaned on these to fill the cracks within my spirit. Over time, though, my sense of self began to break down, until I lost myself completely.

My therapist then told me something that shifted everything.

"Maile," she said kindly, "even if you were in the wrong, no one ever deserves to be called names, yelled at and degraded. That's called abuse. You should never have to feel afraid within a relationship."

Those words hung in the air for a minute. They felt…right. My eyes opened to the truth of the situation, as if I could finally step out of the darkness and back into the light. I vowed to renew my meditation practice and mind myself again.

As I did this work, my depression slowly lifted, and my confidence returned. I began to find that inner core of being again. I had always thought women in abusive relationships were weak or cowardly and had little compassion for them. To suddenly realize that I was in a verbally and emotionally abusive relationship rocked my world. It had happened so slowly and insidiously. A small, scared voice in the back of my mind had told me that something wasn't right, but I had been unable to listen.

I often wonder what would have happened to me if not for that therapist and those simple words that saved me from the path I was on.

Ten months after the flood, I stood in a small courtroom before a judge to declare bankruptcy. I had tried to rebuild my home, but had hit an emotional wall I couldn't seem to go around. I had also run out of money, and my credit cards were maxed out. Bankruptcy freed me of both the house and credit cards. There has always been a stigma regarding bankruptcy, and I saw it as a great failure on my part. I also saw no other way out. So, shame and relief sat balanced on my shoulders like great winged birds, the weight of them both heavy, but stabilizing.

A year after the flood I found myself once again in a courtroom. My name is called. I stood, and the judge declared my marriage officially over. I waited for the sadness to come, but only felt relief. Leaving the courtroom, I stepped outside. The sun was out, the air was warm, and I felt free.

I was divorced.
My bankruptcy was complete.
I was no longer burdened by the house.
And I had finally left Dave.

I continued to go to therapy to address my losses and began to find a deep place of strength inside me. I no longer felt like I was spinning out of control, and my depression had lifted. I started nursing school and found a job to support that endeavor. Life was full of possibilities again.

Though I was still laden with scars from that year, I was also holding deeper wells of wisdom and resilience that helped me see the world differently. I saw myself with kinder eyes and understood more fully what I was capable of. My meditation practice had deepened, and I was learning how to hold my pain like a small child, loving it for all it had to offer. There was no end to the love I had received from others, and I was digging into the love I had for myself - of which I was certain there was also no end.

I learned that living is about sitting with all the suffering, emotions, wants, fears, and trauma. If we can simply sit with it all until it gives way, we are left with the most wondrous gentleness towards ourselves. That tenderness then extends to every aspect of our life. I now soften myself, and where I still feel tension, I soften more.

In retrospect, I view the flood as a great gift. My pain and sorrow were gifts as well. When we are in the thick of it; when we are wading through the shit; there is a part of us that comes alive. We only have to stop long enough to listen. If we can, it will whisper to us the story of who we really are.

I watched as the sun illuminated the river running through the city, bridges crossing it in a mosaic of hugs. I took a deep breath. I breathed in the city, the air, the past, the future - and exhaled it all slowly. In that moment, I was whole. I had survived. Even more, I was thriving. And that could never be taken from me.

Maile Ellis

Flooded

It's the drifting that gets old first,

the chaos,

the spinning thoughts,

the fact that no matter where I go I still can't find my home.

Wind swirls beneath me,

a crawl space lit by fans,

a place that I never wanted to climb into

but found myself nonetheless,

covered in mud,

surrounded by darkness,

the damp smell of earth that still clings to my skin.

I long for an anchor

for anything to pull me back down from the drifting.

But when most of your stuff is gone

and your house is reduced to studs and joints,

the gutting happens inside as well.

At least the shock is receding,

the numb wave of fear and loss

that leaves little hope in its wake.

Reality settles in

like a sticky residue you can't clean off

no matter how hard you scrub.

And I am merely an echo of my neighbors,

a pattern down my street,

a member of a community whose eyes are now haunted,

whose hands are bruised and cut,

whose hearts are still under water.

But there is also the undercurrent that we all feel,

the simple strength of our friends, our family,

our city,

that even in the darkest moments

we hear whisper to us-

All is not lost.

You are safe.

We are here.

And like any good action movie,

the hero finds a way to survive

after all.

Maile Ellis

"There are no hopeless situations; there are only men who have grown hopeless about them."

Clare Boothe Luce

Hope or Help

COVID was a time of significant turmoil for many people. But even before COVID, my life was spinning out of control. My brain seemed like it was racing, and my intrusive thoughts were out of control. I was doom scrolling the news and not sleeping. I had severe mental health issues and was depressed and sad. Friendships had become hard work, and nobody was listening anymore. People just seemed to talk at me, rather than to me. I felt unheard and unseen. I began to feel isolated from everyone and withdrew from life. It was a really difficult time. I felt profoundly alone.

The next few months were bleak. It was the darkest time of my entire life. I had fallen out of love with myself. My closest friends became distant. In hindsight, I can see how some of my choices contributed to the disconnect, but the hurt of them pulling away was painful. But other friends appeared out of the darkness. Friends who I didn't know well were able to give me much-needed space and time. Some of them were willing to just listen to me weep and scream. Others lovingly read bedtime stories to help me fall asleep. Some friends shared daily yoga stretches and breathing exercises to practice. Many left me messages of love and encouragement. Several friends spent hours simply talking and listening to me. They walked the excruciating and emotionally painful journey with me. These conversations and gifts of time gave me the help and hope that kept me alive.

I decided to seek professional therapy to help me with my healing. After searching for a while, I was able to find a private counselor. She helped me process my thoughts and see the positive aspects of my life again! Now, five years later, she is still my counselor. She has the ability to soothe me when my emotions get raw. These appointments are emotional anchors for me. She helped me make sense of the gloom and desperation I experienced. One thing she repeatedly said is etched into my brain forever: "When you have either hope or help, it's never the end."

Today life is good again. Love and support sometimes come from the most unexpected places and people. Never stop thanking them. Never stop loving them. They have demonstrated they are your people.

And always, always remember - when you have hope or help, it's never the end.

Deb Watkins

Tough Old Bird

They say, "When it rains, it pours." I learned the year my husband died that sometimes it rains so much you feel you might drown.

Mac was the love of my life. We were married for forty-eight years. We met on a blind date in Grenada in 1971 and were married a year later. Our life together was wonderful. I know a lot of people say that, but for us it was true. Of course, we had disagreements from time to time, but I wouldn't have traded what I had with him for anything.

One day in early 2020 he went to the emergency room for what he thought was pink eye. He didn't have it, but some of their tests revealed he had blood in his urine. The doctor ordered some additional tests, which led to a diagnosis of bladder cancer. He had been having urgency with urination for a while, but thought it was because he was getting older - so he had ignored it. They quickly scheduled him for surgery to remove the tumor, as well as chemotherapy. It was...rough. The treatments were ultimately unsuccessful, and his cancer quickly progressed.

Mac wanted to be at home, surrounded by familiar surroundings and with friends and family. His twin brother came to help and stayed for months at a time. Mac's condition worsened quickly. He had to be helped to the bathroom and have various bags frequently drained and replaced. Toward the end of his life, his legs became black and oozed a lot of fluid. We had to put towels under him to soak up the wet excretions. He was unable to lie down, so he slept upright in a chair. It was heart-wrenching and excruciating to watch. It was also physically and emotionally exhausting.

Through it all, Mac was optimistic. He didn't complain but was grateful for the love and assistance. Though I offered options for natural approaches to support him, he wasn't interested. He wanted to do it his own way. It was challenging to see him suffering and not be able to help him, but I did my best to be there for him the way he wanted.

My sweet husband died in March 2021. It was like losing a piece of my heart. I was profoundly sad. Thankfully, my friends and family wrapped me in love. It made a difference. The wonderful stories people shared about his impact on their lives were so healing. One lady even told me she had been planning to kill herself, but after a brief conversation with Mac decided not to follow through on her plans. He just had that kind of effect on people. The stories that poured in were like a healing balm to my broken heart. To know he was so well loved was evidence that he had left the world better for having been here. That was an enormous comfort to me.

Two weeks after Mac passed away, I had another blow. The

building which housed the two businesses we co-owned, called 'Rocks and Locks,' was struck by a car. He was a master locksmith and ran the 'locks' side of the business. Though it was my 'baby,' we both shared the 'rocks' side of the business, in which we procured and sold crystals, stones and unique rocks from all over the world. While the building itself was insured, none of the products were. Over one-hundred thousand dollars of merchandise was destroyed.

Insurance paid for the repair of the building, and six months later we re-opened. However, six months after that the store manager died. I had to close the locksmith side of the business. I soon learned that the manager had been stealing from us. I felt an enormous sense of betrayal. I had thought of him as a brother. Learning of his theft only added to my already suffocating grief.

In the midst of it all, my sister was also suffering from severe dementia. She would often call me to ask if I was in heaven. These phone calls were difficult. I felt a great deal of compassion for her, and yet I was running on emotional fumes. Everything felt difficult and seemed to take more energy than I felt like I had.

I continued to run the rock side of the business - until in 2022 the building was once again hit by a car. It was just too much, so I closed the business permanently.

I've been asked, how was I able to get through that painful time?

On reflection, I think we're all stronger than we realize. That strength often makes itself known when confronted with the choice to fold up - or stand up and keep going. I was scared, sad, numb, and overwhelmed. But life was irrevocably going on all around me. The world had not stopped spinning, and I had obligations I couldn't ignore. There were finances to sort out; bills to pay; employees to pay (before I closed the business); and other business obligations. I knew I couldn't just shut down. I had been raised to be a strong and capable person. I also wanted to make Mac and my belated father proud of me. So, I handled things - because that is all I knew how to do.

Fifteen months after Mac's passing, I finally had a Celebration of Life service. I still miss him every day, but I feel his presence all the time. I see him in the eyes of people whose lives he touched. I see him in the love and laughter when people share stories about him. I see him in the auction purchases he made over the years that I am still sorting through. And some may think it is just my imagination, but I also saw him in the Heron that randomly showed up in my driveway, miles from any body of water. I felt his presence when the solar lights shined, even though there was no sunshine for days to charge them. And I experienced his presence at midnight once when the deck camera alarm sounded. I peeked out the window to see an ethereal being in the driveway, surrounded by light, wearing his signature ball cap waving at me. These assurances comfort me.

Life can still be challenging, and I still keenly feel the loss of Mac and my beloved business. But I also have faith in the universe, my friends, and myself. I know that no matter what happens I will be okay. As my employees have said to me in the past, "Marie, you're a tough old bird." Yes, I am. I kinda like that!

Mac liked that about me too.

Marie Andersen-Whitehurst

"Hopelessness has surprised me with patience."

Margaret J. Wheatley

Walking Out Of The Darkness

I still remember waking up the morning after. My body felt like lead. My head pounded and my throat was dry as a desert. I couldn't stop replaying the night before in my mind.

I hadn't slept well. I didn't sleep well most nights anyway, plagued by nightmares that replayed the multitude of traumas I'd witnessed or experienced. I was lucky to sleep more than four hours consecutively, and most nights I slept for two hours before waking up in a cold sweat, heart pounding, mind racing.

I couldn't lie in bed all day. I knew enough to know that would make it worse. Reluctantly, I forced myself out of bed and shuffled downstairs.

My old dog met me at the bottom of the stairs. Miss Cricket had turned eleven a few weeks before; she didn't climb the stairs anymore, and she couldn't hike my mountain because the trail was too hard, but she loved to walk and wander the woods with me. She taught herself how to scent track and how to take me home again safely, even if it was dark outside. She was too old to do search and rescue, but she liked this game of finding home, so I let her play, and I learned to trust her.

I didn't want to go out. I wanted to stay in bed, and if I couldn't do that I wanted to sit on the couch and watch movies all day. I wanted to be alone, and at the same time I couldn't be alone with the thoughts in my head.

But Miss Cricket begged for a walk, pacing back and forth from the door to her bed next to my desk. She didn't bark at me, just paced, grumbled, and pleaded in the way that dogs know best.

I got up and put on my boots. She didn't need a leash where we were walking - she knew the way better than I, and she never went far from me. Even though she was starting to go deaf, she always knew when I called. We went out, across the backyard, and down the bank to the old railroad bed.

It was a beautiful July morning in Maine. It was sunny and clear, warm but not too oppressively hot, and the whole world was alive with summertime. The wildflowers, in full bloom, smelled like heaven. The air was heavy with the sound of bumblebees working over the blackberry brambles alongside the old pasture road we walked.

I could not appreciate any of it.

I was still stuck, somewhere inside my head, in a place I did not know but yet, had lived for over half my life.

I once thought Post Traumatic Stress Disorder was something that happened to soldiers, not to kids. At this point several professionals have speculated that I likely developed PTSD when I was about twelve years old, although I was not diagnosed until I was in my twenties and the symptoms developed into the sleeplessness and nightmares that impacted my job. Reading through the diagnostic criteria for PTSD, over the years I have experienced nearly every symptom in the book.

I thought, that July morning, that I was just dealing with more of the same. Sure, the night before I'd worked a scene for hours. A friend of mine had died. When the call had come in, I knew I was the only member of my fire department in town that evening, and I knew who we were going to see, and I knew it was going to be bad.

But I wasn't actually alone. Two others were just coming into town when the call came in, and I arrived at the scene after them. I didn't have to do much besides keep the area clear while the others did their job. It wasn't as bad as some calls; at least here, I hadn't tried to save anyone. We knew that my friend was already far beyond our help. It wasn't like the day I cleaned the blood out of my mother's hair in the emergency room, or the night I laid on the side of the road next to a kid who'd been hit by a vehicle, trying to keep him safe until someone else could help. It wasn't that bad, actually, and I was just doing my job. I should have been fine.

Or so I told myself, as I trudged along the old gravel road

behind my dog. I should have been fine.

The pasture road was overgrown from what it was when I was a child. Thin birch saplings spread lacey fingers into the walkway and white pines pop up like spindly little bottle brushes underfoot. What was once wide enough for trucks and farm equipment was now a little footpath, with a row of trees to the right between the pasture and I, and to the left, a densely-forested hill climbing upwards.

At a break in the trees, the pasture opened up to our right. Cricket bounced off, chasing a smell. As an Airedale terrier, she is a hunting dog by breed and a tracking dog by nature. I never knew what she was chasing, but I knew she wouldn't go too far from me. I stepped off the road into the old pasture, treading wildflowers under my feet and pushing through the blackberry brambles as I followed her.

A half-dozen yards into the pasture I stopped and stood still. My chest was as heavy as a stone and my breath felt pinched, like I was breathing in through a tiny straw. My heart pounded - not fast, but deep, hurting and breaking. I felt my own pulse, expecting to feel the little butterflies of tachycardia, but instead finding a heavy stone falling into the river with each beat of my heart.

Three hundred feet away, Miss Cricket stopped chasing her scent trail. She turned back, eyes tracking along the treeline. When she saw me, her ears perked up and she bounced before running back through the overgrown pasture towards me.

I never called to her, but she came, flying through the wildflowers like a ray of sunshine.

A few weeks later I had another panic attack, this time during a training exercise. I had been trying to work through the pain, because that was all I knew to do and because that usually worked, but this time the hurt was too deep and the damage was too great. I wasn't sleeping, and I wasn't eating well. I struggled to get through the bare minimum of my work commitments and I isolated myself from my family, from my fire department, from my friends. I just needed to work through it, I told myself.

And then I couldn't work anymore.

I needed help.

Thankfully, I had people who had my back. I was lost, helpless and hopeless, but there were people around me who refused to lose me. One of my firefighters found a counselor I could debrief with, and helped me find a therapist I could see regularly. I ended up being placed on medication to treat post traumatic stress by suppressing the adrenaline response while I slept, so for the first time in years I could sleep through the night. I started an intense therapy treatment with a therapist who worked as a first responder and understood the job.

In our first session, she asked me to visualize a place where I felt safe - maybe a waterfall, or my mountain trails - and to imagine a stop sign at an intersection. To one side of the road was the panic, and to the other was the safe place. She asked me to visualize that stop sign and to turn towards the safe place every time I felt the pressure building in my chest that signaled the panic attack coming on.

To my dismay, as I searched through my mind, there were no physical places where I felt safe, and no imaginary places either. I did not know how to feel safe, and I began to understand that I hadn't known how to feel safe since I was a child.

Instead of a place, I found safety in a single moment. A year before, as a newly licensed EMT, just cleared to run calls with my volunteer fire department, I'd responded to a medical emergency alone. I was terrified of failure, of doing it alone without someone holding my hand, but I went out to do the job I'd been trained for.

The transporting ambulance arrived on scene seconds before me, so I was not responsible for taking care of the patient. I assisted the other crew as much as they needed, and then I cleared the scene. I drove back to the station and navigated the complex maneuver of backing my ambulance into the station between the other trucks, and as I turned off the truck, all of the station lights clicked on.

I wasn't sure what had happened, but as I climbed out of the truck I saw one of my officers standing in the back of the bay. He had heard me take the call, and even though he wasn't running medical calls, he had left home and driven over to the area. He waited, where I couldn't see his truck, until I cleared the scene; then he moved so I couldn't see him, and followed me back to the station at a distance.

"It was my first call," I told him, trying to stop my hands from shaking. My stomach felt like lead.

"I know," he said. "You did good. I wanted you to do it yourself, but I wanted to be there in case you needed help."

Standing there in the truck bay, his words stopped the trembling in my hands, and a warmth replaced the lead in my belly. I felt safe. And it wasn't a bubble-wrapped, nothing-will-ever-go-wrong kind of safety; it was simply the realization that I didn't have to do it alone anymore, even if I was on my own.

That was the first time in a very long time that I felt safe. At the time, it was just a flicker of hope, just a passing moment. As I searched my thoughts to find something - anything - that said 'safe', I found that little flicker.

Thirty seconds became a lifeline.

I used that moment to recover. The stop sign my therapist talked about became very real, the intersection at the end of my road, with a left turn towards my station and that feeling of safety, and a right turn towards the bad call and the panic.

Every time that the pressure built in my chest and that my thoughts began racing, in my mind, I took the left-hand turn. In that space, I found silence instead of the non-stop noise that had filled my brain for years.

I began, slowly, to heal.

I walked with Miss Cricket. We walked miles almost every day, just the two of us. Instead of the soundtrack of trauma in my mind, I listened to music and to audiobooks. I listened to the birds overhead. I listened to the waterfall and the river. I hiked, and walked, and slept, and ate, and I learned how to set boundaries and how to not overwork myself to drown out the noise. I set goals and made better choices that aligned with my goals, including a career change that would allow me more time off to take care of myself. I met the love of my life - I knew he was the one when I realized he didn't give me butterflies in my stomach, but instead that same safe and secure feeling that I'd learned to value.

With my old girl beside me, and with so many people having my back, I walked my way back out of the darkness.

As I write this, Cricket is asleep beside my desk. She is quite old now, and reaching the end of her own journey. A few weeks ago, my therapist told me that I no longer meet the clinical criteria for an active PTSD diagnosis. Something in me is intensely grateful that she lived long enough to see this transformation. A young pup sleeps in his bed near us; he is my therapy dog in training, learning how to walk others out of the darkness too.

Annie Louise Twitchell

"Loss of hope rather than loss of life is what decides the issues of war. But helplessness induces hopelessness."

B.H. Liddell Hart

Billy's Gift

Stay open to the possibility that when your world shatters, it is not the end. Even though it's the end of life as you know it, it's not the end of a life that is still to be created and lived.

I know it may sound like I am minimizing pain and suffering, but please hear me out. Staying open to hope, while recognizing and honoring our pain can be our saving grace. It has the potential to heal us in ways we don't see or expect.

It did for me.

My husband, Billy, was away on a business trip when I was awakened from a sound sleep by the telephone. I immediately knew something was very wrong. I was informed Billy had stopped breathing. They were waiting for an ambulance. The fear on the other line was palpable. I was also terrified. My brain refused to accept what this might mean, but my physical body "knew." I immediately started to shake violently. My body felt like it had been suddenly plunged into a deep freeze. My mind was racing with anxiety, yet paradoxically numb. Nothing made sense. I had just kissed him goodbye that morning, fully expecting him to return the next day. Now he wasn't breathing! It was too horrible to contemplate.

An hour later, my phone rang again. Heart pounding, I answered. The ER doctor told me "I'm sorry to be the one to tell you this, but your husband is dead." My world fell apart. A gaping hole in my life immediately opened, and I plunged into an abyss of abject grief.

It was too much for me to grasp. He was only 58 years old and had just passed his annual physical exam with flying colors. He was in the prime of his life! But he had also been under immense stress - far more than he had told me. The pressure had quickly and silently built inside his body like a powder keg ready to blow. That night it shattered his beautiful heart. Now the warmth and vitality of his brilliant smile, his comforting touch, and the sound of his voice were forever gone.

Until then, I had felt lucky to not yet have been directly touched by familial death. My parents were, however, getting older. As their primary caregiver, I was concerned about their health and longevity. My mother was in her late seventies, and my father was in his early eighties. My father had just come through bypass surgery a few months earlier. I was starting to brace myself for the possibility they wouldn't be around much longer. I wanted to be prepared, so I searched for ways to help navigate the eventual loss. Books, poems and memes about death and loss frequently crossed my path. I bought, read, and saved most of them. My hope was that they would ease the process of grief when it inevitably happened.

I never thought my husband would die before my parents. I

never imagined all those saved nuggets of wisdom were printed with the invisible ink of his name rather than those of my parents.

I would become exceedingly familiar with the kind of loss that shook me to the absolute core of my being. Thankfully, the insights I had gathered did help me navigate the devastating loss of my precious husband. And they often imbued me with hope when I most needed encouragement. They were lights in the dark.

Three days after his death, I finally posted about my loss on Facebook. I wasn't sleeping well and had been waking up between 2:00 and 3:00 every morning. Tears streamed down my face as I was overtaken with a strange and unexpected desire to write. I needed to share our story. I needed to grieve publicly, but from the safety of my grief cocoon.

That first early morning post opened a space to share about his life, as well as our life together. Although I did not realize it yet, this sharing was the remarkable means that would enable me to crawl up and out of the abyss of grief that consumed me. I felt absolutely compelled to write. The words came as a veritable stream of consciousness. These grief essays weren't long, but writing and sharing them with the world brought a small glimmer of hope during my despair. Sharing each story was akin to opening little pressure valves that released streams of pent-up trauma. I always felt better afterward and could sometimes even fall back into a more restful sleep.

My written words were raw, sometimes full of typos, misspelled words, and imperfect grammar. But every word was heartfelt, gut-wrenching, and authentic. It was a visceral experience, a poetic keening from my soul.

The stories kept pouring out of me. It became a ritual each morning. I would wake up, write, post, and grieve. As I continued to write, I discovered a new voice and a creative path out of the darkness. My sharing developed into a deep gratitude for all who read, commented, and encouraged me. It was an unexpected gift. It was a way to help myself grieve in a manner that felt kind to myself.

Writing allowed me to process my feelings, to show vulnerability, to embrace my fear, and to recognize that I was stronger than I knew. It helped me realize I could get through hardship and tough times - including this one.

I later compiled all the essays to share in a book. I was encouraged to publish, but I'm not sure I will do so. The memory of Billy's death is still painful, but I'm not sure that I want or need to publish the essays anymore. They did the work that was needed at the time. Maybe that is enough.

I feel immense gratitude for having come through, and emerged out of, the abyss. The experience left me a bit battered, but more whole in some vital ways. I am stronger for processing his death in my own way. Staying present with the experience, while having confidence in my ability to creatively process hard things was my saving grace. To see my own strength and resilience through writing has been a true gift. Indeed, it was the best and last gift he gave me. The gift of writing. I intend to nurture and develop this gift as I continue to grow, love, and process my losses in life.

Writing has not only helped me on my healing journey, but also allowed me to creatively use all the shattered pieces of my life to create a beautiful mosaic.

I am profoundly grateful.

Susan Johnson-Smith

"To live without hope is to cease to live."

Fyodor Dostoevsky

A Time To Live

She wasn't supposed to be coming yet. It was three and a half months before she was due to arrive. Our baby was being born far too soon, and we were terrified.

My wife, Beth, and I had been in Pasadena, California for three weeks for a pastor's conference. I was the pastor for two congregations in Central Illinois at the time. The obstetrician had cleared Beth for travel, since she was low-risk and well within the permissible window for safe traveling for pregnant women. While in Pasadena, however, Beth began to spike a fever and experience mild to moderate contractions. We called the doctor, who assured us that everything was likely fine, and that Beth probably just needed to rest. Things didn't seem to progress, so we traveled back home to Illinois.

After we arrived, the contractions increased in severity, becoming strong and frequent. We called the obstetrician, who initially advised us to come into the office, then changed their minds when they remembered Beth was not even six months pregnant. He then told her to take two 'stiff belts of whiskey' to try to stop the contractions. That didn't work, so the doctor told us to get to the hospital. We lived out in the country, traveling on remote, ill-kept, rough roads. We bumped our way into town, the contractions exacerbated by every pothole and patch-worked stretch of road. When we arrived, the doctor tried to medically stop the contractions, however it finally became evident that it was not working. This baby was coming.

The air was ripe with the feeling of dread and doom. The doctor and nurses tried to prepare us for the inevitability that our baby would be born alive but would die within minutes. The prospect was gut wrenching. There is a verse in the book of Ecclesiastes that says, "There is a time to be born and a time to die". This was the time our baby would be born. We hoped it was not also the time our baby would die.

They had transferred Beth to the operating room, and amazingly I was allowed to accompany her. I will be forever grateful for that gift because what I witnessed will be forever etched into my memory. Our daughter, Sharran, was born with one eye open and one eye shut - shaking her tiny fist in the air. It was as if she was saying, "It's not time for me to be born, and I don't want to be born yet, but I will make it work and do the best I can!"

They quickly showed our baby to Beth, and then the doctor and I RAN to the neonatal ICU with Sharran to hook her up to the machines that would hopefully save her life.

The following week, the entire medical staff, including doctors, nurses, and respiratory therapists, continually consoled and comforted us about the death of our baby - who was still alive! It was surreal. And, true to her defiant first pump when she was born, against all odds, she kept on living.

Beth was unable to go to the hospital every day since she had just gone through an extremely traumatic birth experience. I was at the hospital for hours every day for both of us. I would talk to Sharran and gently touch her with olive oil on my fingers. The doctor had told us that the nutrients in olive oil were good for Sharran, and helped reduce any irritation from friction that touch might cause her skin. It was heartbreaking to see my sad looking little baby struggling for her life. When I wasn't at the hospital, I would often run until I was exhausted and numb. The exhaustion helped get things out of my head, if even for a brief time.

Sharran was in a room with other babies who were also hooked up to monitors. When babies are born too early, because of their underdeveloped nervous system, they often 'forget' to breathe. When that happens, monitors alert the nurses. They would then have to isolate the sound to determine which baby was in distress. Once identified, they would place their hand on the baby's chest and gently shake them to remind them to take a breath. I had witnessed this happening a few times while visiting and it began to intrude into my dreams at night.

I had recently bought a new scuba watch, which had a temperature alarm. I'm a huge scuba diving enthusiast, so I was very thrilled with my purchase. At the time, we lived in a huge house, which was expensive to heat, so we tended to turn the thermostat down at night while we were sleeping. One night, around three o'clock in the morning, I dreamed that an alarm was going off for one of the babies in the neonatal unit. I dreamed that I looked around for help, but there was no nurse or respiratory therapist to be found. I rushed from child to child trying to figure out which baby was in distress, but finally woke to realize the alarm was coming from my watch, because the temperature in the house had dropped. In my half asleep, traumatized stupor, I couldn't seem to turn the watch alarm off - so I opened the door and threw the watch as far as I could into the cold, wet snow. I didn't care about the watch anymore. I just wanted my baby to be okay.

After a while, the doctors and nurses stopped talking about Sharran's impending death. Instead, they began to voice concerns about her functionality. They said that if she continued to live, she would have massive deficits. These might include blindness, Cerebral Palsy (CP), or a variety of other disabilities. None of those ever manifested, except for the mildest possible CP type symptoms that the untrained eye would never detect or notice. Over the three and a half months Sharran spent in the neonatal ICU, the medical staff was continually astonished at her progress, and eventually began to believe and act like she was going to live.

One of the neonatologists did a brain scan on Sharran. He said the results were 'indeterminate.' He started to say, "If you took one-hundred babies like Sharran…," then he stopped himself and said, "No, that's not true. There are no babies like Sharran. We just don't know. Some areas may be fine, and some not… we don't know."

As it turned out, at one pound, five ounces, Sharran was the smallest baby born in East Central Illinois to survive and thrive until that time. In the next few days, her weight dropped to one pound, two ounces. Now she is in her mid-forties with two kids of her own. She is an occupational therapist who helps others in their healing. Her initial story that seemed to start with 'all hope is gone', morphed into a beautiful, talented and gifted woman.

I'm convinced the tiny, determined fist she shook at the world when she was born was a manifestation of the fighting spirit God gave her to help her survive her abrupt entry into the world.

Rand Holm

"We must accept finite disappointment, but never lose infinite hope."

Martin Luther King, Jr.

Love Heals

Feelings of shock coursed through me like a bolt of lightning as my stepfather's hands slithered under my jacket. At twelve years old, I suddenly found myself in an unexpected and extremely dangerous situation. Ten minutes earlier, he asked if I wanted to sit in front of his motorcycle and drive. I was thrilled with the offer. Now we were on an isolated country road, and I didn't know what to do. I hoped the placement of his hands was some kind of bizarre mistake. Maybe he didn't realize where his hands had come to rest, I rationalized. With one hand I gingerly removed his hands from my breasts, pulling my jacket closed. Seconds later he reached around and opened my jacket again, returning his hands to their former place. I realized at that moment it was not an accident.

I was too afraid to pull over and stop the motorcycle. We were in the middle of nowhere. I felt sick. My gut tightened with fear and disbelief. I continued driving, hoping to get to a more populated area where I could stop and get off.

I honestly don't remember how I got back home, or for how long he kept his hands on me. But that was the beginning of a long and tortuous nightmare. When I got home, I told my mother about it, but she refused to believe me.

He was also physically violent. I was a mere slip of a girl at five feet, two inches tall and barely more than a hundred pounds soaking wet. He was a big man, around six feet, four inches tall. His beatings were severe, and the offense provoking his attacks could be as simple as leaving a glass of water on the table. His preferred instrument for inflicting punishment was a thick, heavy belt.

My mother, who was obsessed with him, quickly learned under his tutelage. She began what we children called "The Round Robin.' If she couldn't figure out which of us had done something she didn't like, she would beat each of us in turn to get a confession. If, at the end of the first round of beatings, one of us hadn't owned up to being the perpetrator, she would start over. It continued until one of us confessed - usually the one who couldn't take the beatings any longer rather than the one who really did it. That child would get one more beating before it was over.

One day my stepfather beat me so severely the school called the police because of the extensive bruises on my body. The police came to school to question me. I told them everything - including about the sexual abuse. During the interview they asked if my stepfather ever beat my mother. I told them he did, even though it wasn't true. I just wanted him to be gone, so I thought if I made it sound worse, it might increase the chance they would make him leave. In the end, however, that lie undermined my credibility. They did come out to the house that night to talk to him and my mother. When my mother told them she had never been beaten, they assumed I had lied about everything, so they left. I was never sure how they explained away the physical bruises.

Instead of leaving my stepfather, my mother made me go live with his brother. He didn't like me very much since I had told the police about my stepfather's abuse. I felt profoundly unloved and unwanted. My mother's rejection also made me extremely vulnerable. The first day at my new school, one of the most popular guys in school expressed interest in me. He was involved in the drug scene. I would have done anything to be accepted and liked, so I also started doing drugs. A lot of drugs. It seemed to help numb the emotional pain that permeated my being. I mostly used weed and LSD, but also barbiturates, speed, and even PCP once. After a hallucinogenic 'trip' that lasted for a few days, I got caught and sent back home.

The beatings and overt sexual abuse stopped when I went back. He was afraid I would report it to the police. Instead, he shifted to touching himself in front of me, self-exposure, innuendo, porn, lascivious looks, and gestures, along with harsh chore related punishments.

In the midst of my anguish at home, I was also severely bullied at school. I was considered a pariah because my sister had a cognitive disability. I often found myself jumping into the fray when other kids were taunting or beating her.

I dreaded going to school - and I dreaded going home. I was

tortured and miserable no matter where I went. There was no safe place. There was no safe person.

So, I ran away.

I was a run-away on the streets of Los Angeles and the surrounding communities for about a month. I encountered many dangerous situations and people - the worst of which were in the safe houses for runaway teens. I barely escaped without being raped, though I was sexually assaulted.

I was finally caught. When they called my mother, she asked if I wanted to come home. I said, 'no.' She told me not to bother then. Nevertheless, I was returned home.

I felt hopeless. I had nobody in my life who loved me. Nobody I could trust. I was considering running again, when a second brother of my stepfather's came to visit from out of state. I had spent a summer with his family a few years earlier and had loved it. He asked if I would like to live with his family. I jumped at the chance.

It was my salvation.

They treated me well. I wasn't used to being able to eat when I was hungry. When I lived with my mother, my oldest sister would steal bologna from the fridge and hide it in her armpit for us to eat when it was safe. I still clearly remember the taste of bologna and sweat. I was shocked that in my new home I was allowed to get something to drink and eat without permission. And though my mother had diamonds on every finger, we often lacked adequate and appropriate clothing. My new 'parents' made sure I was well-dressed, immediately providing me with underwear, clean clothing, a coat, and shoes without holes. Having my basic needs met made me feel extravagantly wealthy! They also treated me with respect and kindness. I wasn't easy to deal with at first, because I was still sneaking drugs, cutting school and shoplifting. But each time I was caught, they dealt with it in a measured and responsible way. After a few months, I settled in, and my self-destructive behaviors began to simply fade away. I even stopped doing drugs. I just lost interest in them. I had more fun going camping, riding horses, swimming and playing tennis with friends. I cut off all ties with my mother after she wrote me a letter telling me the Bible would allow her to stone me to death if she desired because of my 'rebellious ways.' I returned future letters unread, until she simply stopped sending them.

In my new home I had a family, love, and a sense of belonging for the first time in my life. I thrived. My last years of school saw my grades return to straight A's, from the D's and 'F's they had plummeted to when my stepfather entered my life.

As I reached adulthood, I realized there were still lots of deep, hidden wounds that needed to heal. I went to therapy - a LOT of therapy - to unpack and process the abuse I experienced as a child. And the truth is there are still scars. But scars are not only evidence of having been wounded, but also of healing.

I know I was lucky. Not every child is rescued like I was. But it has helped me understand how much difference a person can make in the life of another. That knowledge has been a powerful motivator for me in my life. I know that love heals. I have experienced it. I try to remember and use that understanding to help others heal. For five years I facilitated a support group for women who had experienced trauma in their life. I have given workshops on self-care and healing for years. I became a Doctor of Oriental Medicine and Licensed Acupuncturist, specializing in treating emotional concerns. I have authored several books on emotional healing, self-care, and the power of self-acceptance and kindness.

The power of love is healing. The family that took me in was far from perfect. There were even some ugly secrets I didn't learn about until I was an adult. But I do know they treated me with kindness and love. It changed my life forever. And when we extend love, even in our own imperfection, it can change lives. It can give hope to someone when they may feel like all hope is gone.

It did for me.

Diane Gross

Hope in Something

"You're a worthless piece of sh*t just like your father!" my mother screamed. For as long as I could remember, I had heard her spew those words at me. I believed her and spent years self-sabotaging in a perverse effort to prove her right.

Home was a chaotic and unsafe place. My mother was a raging alcoholic who was often physically and verbally abusive. A stream of men she brought home from bars came in and out of our lives. She was married five times. They weren't 'top-shelf' choices. My biological father was not only an alcoholic and drug addict, but he was also a career criminal. He had been in prison several times for various illegal activities, including forgery and armed robbery.

I began drinking and smoking weed when I was twelve years old. My friends and I would also go into the wood-shop lacquer room to get high off fumes. I now realize that the euphoric high I sought was to help numb my emotional pain.

My grandmother was the light of my life. We always lived near her, and I considered her more a mother to me than my own. She was always there for me. I didn't realize at the time what a pivotal role she would end up playing in my life. Her love, and the intense desire to not disappoint her sometimes kept me sane.

My life was chaotic and unstable, so I was a prime target for predators. I was sexually abused by numerous men from the age of six until I was fourteen. The whispered words, "I love you," made me feel special, as did the lavish gifts, movies, and treats. They often showed me affection and took time to listen to me. The sexual abuse didn't seem like such a bad trade-off at the time. It had been happening for so long, I had come to see it as 'normal.' By the time I was fourteen, however, I couldn't tolerate it anymore. I became violent with the man who was abusing me at the time. He never tried again.

In 1979, when I started junior high school, I began working with a band as a 'roadie'. I helped load the van and set up the equipment. It was exciting to be doing something so 'cool.' I desperately wanted to fit-in. Being part of the band made me feel important. It was glorious.

Everyone in the band drank heavily. I had easy access, so I also drank - a lot. During the nine years I worked with them, I regularly used cocaine and methamphetamine. I was high and drunk almost all the time. My life started to spiral out of control, and I attempted suicide several times.

By 1988 my drug addiction was out of control. I began to inject heroin from time to time. My physical appearance started to reflect the pummeling my body was taking from the drugs and alcohol. It became bad enough that some of the band members expressed concern. In the wake of the conflict that arose, I quit. I tried living with my father, but that quickly fell apart, so I returned home to my mother's house.

I couldn't sustain attending school and doing the required work, so I dropped out in the eleventh grade. I got a job as a telemarketer and moved out of my mother's house. On my own, my life was a constant 'party.' My drug use quickly escalated. I got into a relationship for a while, but I loved cocaine more than I loved her, so it didn't last.

I started working with another band. My addiction became extreme. I lost my home and was arrested. My memory of that time is so hazy I don't even remember the exact charges, but it had something to do with screaming and verbal abuse. I was let off easily with community service.

Now homeless, I ping-ponged between living in my car and staying with my grandmother. I didn't want my grandmother to see how bad my alcohol and drug use had become, so I used more sparingly when I was around her. I didn't want to disappoint her. Though I continued to circle the drain, for a long time she was the one that kept me from completely going down it.

The next few years were a blur of bad decisions; bad relationships; sleeping with hookers; getting hired - and inevitably fired. I was shooting-up a lot of heroin and cocaine multiple times a day. I was still drinking and using a variety of other drugs, as well. Things inevitably started to unravel. Every door in my life began to shut. People didn't want me in their homes because I brought chaos with me. I was unsafe, unpredictable, and untrustworthy. My life was utterly and completely broken.

My life took its first upward turn in 1998. A friend talked me into entering a short detox program with him. A lot of people were dying from heroin overdose at the time. I agreed. After detox, however, I started using again almost immediately. I overdosed and almost died three times that week. I knew I had to do something. I was 'sick and tired of being sick and tired,' so I checked myself into a one-hundred-day rehabilitation program. I've been sober ever since.

During the years addiction controlled my life, I had spurts of 'hope,' but it was always misdirected. I drank and used drugs because I hoped it would numb my pain. I moved from place to place in hopes of getting a fresh start. I entered into new relationships, hoping happiness would magically appear. I hoped a new job would stabilize my life. None of it worked. It couldn't. I hoped some external change was somehow going to fix my life. I didn't understand that 'wherever you go, there you are.' I wasn't changing the very thing that needed to change - me. The only real hope for lasting change is internal change.

I've learned it's important to make sure we place our hope in the right thing. It will save a lot of time and prevent a lot of suffering. My own path might have been drastically different if I had placed my hope in my 'higher power,' or in people who attempted to help me; or in the possibility of healing my emotional wounds instead of numbing them. Still, I know having hope in something, even misplaced hope, can nevertheless keep us from giving up. It can keep us trying, even as we stumble in the dark. It kept me alive until I was able to find my way. I have been sober since 1998.

Nick C.

"If you're going through hell, keep going,"

Winston Churchill

Courage to Change

The first time I had a drink was when I was about six years old. The grownups were having a party, and I was making my way around the room finishing off what was left in the glasses. I liked how it felt. From that moment, I drank whenever I could. I snuck sips from the bottles on the countertop and fridge. As time went on I began to isolate myself from my sisters so they didn't smell the alcohol on my breath.

Drinking on the down-low continued until I was fifteen years old. That's when I got married. My husband was already of legal drinking age, so alcohol was readily available, and so I drank - a lot. I also started to use crank and amphetamines along with alcohol. I quickly discovered my husband was gay. It felt like a gut punch. I was angry, hurt and confused. I was only fifteen years old and not emotionally equipped to be able to navigate this kind of situation. I felt alone and unloved. I tried to remedy that by sleeping around. It, of course, didn't work.

I finally left my husband when I was twenty-two years old. By that time alcohol and drugs were an integral part of my life. I moved in with a man who was still married but separated from his wife. He didn't like me doing drugs, so I tried to control and hide my use as much as I could. I was also spiraling emotionally. I was deeply depressed and suicidal. My live-in boyfriend and I shared the same birthday. When he decided to go spend the day with his family, I was convinced that he wanted to leave me and go back to them. I wanted so badly to be loved and accepted. My mother didn't want me. My dad had disowned me. And now I was convinced my boyfriend wanted to leave me too. I decided to 'leave' him before he left me. I was determined to end my life. I downed two bottles of aspirin. It didn't kill me though, it just made me violently ill.

I decided to leave. I called my mother and my stepfather, Dean, to ask if I could stay with them for a while. They agreed. I packed my things, got on a bus, and left. Mother, who struggled with mental illness, was in the hospital when I arrived, so Dean picked me up. Instead of going home, he took me to a bar. I started drinking. When we got home, he raped me.

I felt dirty and degraded. I drank to numb the shame and pain. That only made things worse. It robbed me of any remaining sense of dignity. When my mother returned home, she and Dean decided to pimp me out. I forced myself to do it a few times but couldn't keep doing it. So, they made me leave.

I started buying a lot of drugs and alcohol at a local strip bar. I met a guy there that seemed nice. We moved in together after a brief period. Then, I caught him having sex on the living room couch. I had to get out. I left and went to a hotel. As I sat in the hotel, I realized that I had no idea what I was going to do or where I was going to live. I didn't even know how I was going to pay the hotel bill. I had no job; no skills; and no money.

I once again decided to kill myself. I called my mother to say goodbye. She got in the car and drove to Santa Cruz, where I was and somehow found the hotel. The manager called 911. The rescue team broke in and found me. As they tried to resuscitate me, my heart stopped, but they were able to revive me. In my drugged state, I heard someone say, "Dumb bitch! What did you want to do that for?" They transported me to the hospital, and I was put on a seventy-two-hour psych hold.

They called my dad, but he didn't want to deal with it. My mother told me I could come back and stay with her if I wanted. I told the hospital that if they released me, I would kill myself. Nevertheless, they released me into the care of my mother.

Not long after that I met my next husband, Brent. I started drinking and doing drugs with increasing frequency - especially after we married. Then I got pregnant. My baby, Karla Ann, was born dead seven months into the pregnancy. I was devastated. My solution, of course, was to double down on my drinking and drugging to numb my pain.

As time went on, I had two children - both born alive. But I was not able to be a good mother to them because of my addiction. We had started to spend a lot more time with Brent's family, and they drank and snorted a lot, so it was a comfortable fit. But my kids suffered. Looking back, I honestly don't even know who was taking care of the kids when we were all getting drunk and high. I regret it so very much.

There were spurts of trying to climb out of my crazy life from time to time. During one such time I decided to go back to school to get my high school diploma. I had only finished sixth grade, and felt education might help improve my life choices. As usual, I got sidetracked when I met - you guessed it! A man. I left my husband, Brent, for him. It was like jumping from the frying pan into the fire. He was a heavy drug and alcohol user and would get mean when he was drunk or high. He liked to hit me. More than once my body and face told the story of his violent temper. Sometimes I would yell for help, but nobody was willing to intervene. I often had to run and/or hide in fear for my life.

Our life was much like a Lifetime movie drama. We drank and did drugs. He was in and out of jail. We lost every apartment we had because of his violence or our inability to pay our rent. He wouldn't work, and so we subsisted on my work as a housekeeper and eventually as a maintenance engineer. But it was never enough money - especially with the price of alcohol and drugs for two addicts. We stayed with his grandmother for a while, but eventually she asked us to leave because her daughter was coming to visit, and she didn't want her daughter to know she was supporting us.

We had nowhere to go. We rode the lite rail. As I sat there watching the landscape rush by, I realized so too was my life rushing by - and yet I was going nowhere. I didn't even have a place to live. Something shifted inside me, and I decided that I needed to get him help. I didn't think I had a problem, but he had one. I talked him into going to an AA meeting. I convinced him that it was for me, and I just needed him to go with me for support. He told me he would go once, but not to expect more. I figured if I could just get him there, someone might say or do something that would make him want to go back. In the end, I stayed. He didn't. Someone said something that made me realize that I had a problem. I decided to get sober. That made him angrier than usual.

At this point, we were homeless. I remember telling God that if he would help me find a place to live, I wouldn't stay in the relationship. I called my mother once again for help. She agreed to let me stay with her for a short time. Her apartment wasn't a particularly safe place, but it was better than the streets. Every day I searched for an apartment. I finally found an apartment that I thought I would be able to afford - IF I could pass the screening. We didn't have a great history of paying for our rent and had been evicted several times. I decided to just be honest with the apartment manager. I told her I was trying to get out of an abusive relationship, and that I was working on my sobriety. She took a chance on me and gave me the apartment. I immediately left him and struck out for the first time in my life on my own.

I continued to focus on staying sober and kept going to AA. I remember my sponsor telling me that I had to put as much time into working the program as I had put into my addiction. So, I did. And that made all the difference.

I've been sober now for over thirty years. It hasn't always been easy, but it has been worth it. Still, after all this time, I am still working to repair the damage caused by my choices and addictive lifestyle. I'll never be able to change the fact that I wasn't there for my kids like they needed and deserved, but I try to be there for them now as much as I can. I can't ever reclaim the lost opportunities the drugs and alcohol took, but I can live life as well as I can today.

The title of this book is 'When All Hope is Gone - What Then?' My answer? When all hope is gone, I pray the AA prayer: "GOD grant me the serenity to accept the things I cannot change, courage to change the things I can, and wisdom to know the difference."

I think it's honestly addressing the second part of the prayer, "…courage to change the things I can…" that made the biggest difference in me getting sober.

Positive change creates hope.

Sharon Flatt

The Dream

The dreams had been shattering my sleep every night for years. The theme was always the same: a faceless man who I knew would rape and kill me if he caught me. My nights were spent running. Always running - through dark streets, abandoned buildings, and dense forests shrouded in thick, suffocating fog. I would wake up in stark terror and panic, my body slamming bolt upright in bed, eyes bulging with fear, heart pounding, and sweat pouring down my body.

Sleep was not the sweet, inviting laze of slumber I desperately needed. Instead, it was a time of dread. I was being relentlessly pursued on a nightly basis. I was prey.

I was familiar with what it was like to be prey. I had grown up learning to duck, run away and hide from my stepfather. He was constantly trying to corner me; to catch me alone; to hurt me. I was too little to fight back, so running seemed like the only option. Years later, he was tormenting my dreams. I couldn't see his face, but I knew it was him.

I despaired of ever being free of him. I felt like I'd never be able to stop running. The dreams were not only affecting my sleep, but also my awake time. I was exhausted from the lack of sleep, as well as the emotional toil the dreams were having. I felt hopeless.

I sought therapy to help me deal with the unhealed trauma I believed was the underlying cause of the disturbing dreams. It had become clear I was still running from what had happened to me as a child. During our sessions, my therapist and I discussed the role of fear. Fear can motivate us to take actions that help keep us safe when there is danger, but unbridled, chronic fear can steal joy and destroy our life. We can remain stuck in fear, even when the real danger is past. However, chronic fear is like a bully. Its power begins to collapse when confronted. Facing fear that has consumed our life is an act of courage. When we are willing to face fear, we gain access to personal power we never imagined was within us. Our discussions provided life support to the hope inside that I had previously thought dead.

Then one night I had 'The Dream.'

I went to bed the night of 'The Dream' like every other night - scared. As I lay there that night, dreading what was to come, for some reason my fear morphed into anger. I felt a sense of rage that he still had power over me. I resented his intrusion into the deepest part of my subconscious - my dreams. I wondered what might happen if I turned and fought back in my dream. The thought left a smile on my face as I drifted off to sleep.

And I dreamed...

He was dressed completely in black, draped in an old trench coat and a battered, brimmed hat drawn low over his brow. The only part of his face I could see was his eyes. They were deep-set, penetrating, and evil. I could sense his sneer and see the threat in his stance. He moved slightly in my direction. I thought, "Oh, God. Please no." I knew with absolute certainty his intention was to hurt me. My throat constricted, my heart raced, and my body tensed. I knew he could sense my fear, for I heard his low, malevolent chuckle. He began moving towards me. I backed away, terrified. Encouraged by my obvious fear, he began to run in my direction. I turned and fled in a panic. He laughed cruelly as he pursued me. Then, inexplicably something inside me snapped. I stopped dead in my tracks. I turned slowly and was surprised to find that he too had stopped and was eyeing me warily. Suddenly, a furious scream erupted from the depths of my being, and I found myself running full speed toward him. His eyes widened in shock, and he turned tail and fled. "CHICKEN," I repeatedly screamed at his retreating figure. "CHICKEN!"

"Diane, wake-up! Are you okay?" My husband was leaning over me, with concern written on his face. I smiled, answering "Yes, I'm okay. I'm gonna be just fine." I smiled again and snuggled deeper into my down comforter and fell into a deep, wonderfully dreamless sleep.

I never had that dream again.

Diane Gross

"Hope is the dream of a waking man."

Aristotle

Desperate Hope

I had grown familiar with the gnaw of hunger in my belly. There were times we had no food, not even rice to eat. Life used to be easy and carefree, but things we had once taken for granted were now uncertain, including food. I remember waiting for dad to come home, desperately hoping he would bring some food. Sometimes we were lucky. Often, though, he came home empty-handed.

My childhood in India, where I grew up, was a happy time for my two older sisters and myself, until I was in seventh grade. My father worked as a Road Transportation Agent (RTA), which is similar to a person who conducts the driver skills test at the Department of Motor Vehicles in the United States. My mother was a homemaker. Together they created a home that felt safe and nurturing. Then my father lost his job. He had enjoyed working at the same place for many years, and suddenly it was gone. The competition for work was fierce, and finding another job wasn't easy - especially one that was satisfying and brought in enough money for a family of five. While Dad did the best he could, it was hard on him. I could see that he was sad and struggling emotionally with the loss.

My mother had to start working. That was difficult for everyone. She would get up early in the morning to cook us breakfast, work a full day, often not getting home till nine o'clock in the evening. I tried to get dinner ready so she wouldn't have to cook, but sometimes that wasn't possible. She was exhausted all the time. It was hard on us too. We were used to having her home. I know it was difficult for my dad to see her working so hard.

My mother worked at her sister's store selling watches. It was unfamiliar work for her, but she did her best. Still, money was extremely tight. I remember the humiliation of being called out publicly at school for late tuition. I was told if we didn't pay soon, I would no longer be welcome to attend. Somehow my mother came through and we were allowed to stay in school.

Life grew to be a day-to-day struggle to survive. I was getting a harsh lesson in what it means to be poor. Sometimes not even our most basic needs were met. One of my sisters even went to live with our aunt to help relieve my family's financial strain.

After I finished college, I began to search for a job. I wanted to help my family. The culture in India, where I grew up, is quite different than in the United States. Parents support and take care of their children until the children are established and stable, then the children support and take care of their parents. It isn't that the children feel an obligation to pay back their parents, rather it is a way to show honor and respect. I had a dream to someday pay off the burden of debt that had accumulated during our struggle to survive. The only job openings I could find in my field, however, were for nightshift work, at minimum wage. I knew such a job could never lead to a lucrative or worthwhile career.

My father encouraged me to get a master's degree. He believed settling for a low-paying local job would limit my future prospects. He told me he would figure out a way to help with the student loans and was willing to even ask his mother for help. I secretly questioned my father's ability to support me in any real, practical way. He was struggling just to provide for our day-to-day needs. Nevertheless, I appreciated his desire to help.

There were enormous hurdles to getting a master's degree. I wasn't certain how I could accomplish it but decided to take the risk. I knew if I could reach this goal, it would change not only my life, but the lives of my entire family.

My mind began to entertain an exciting, but terrifying possibility. What if I got my master's and pursued a career in the United States? I knew of people who had helped their entire family climb out of the pits of poverty in that way.

Hope, mixed with a generous spattering of fear, sprang up inside me. Something inside of me knew I had to do it. I also knew I had to succeed. Failure was not an option. There was too much at stake. The burden of responsibility, however, felt enormous.

There were many hoops I had to jump through before I would

be allowed to come to the United States for school. There were tests to pass, and documents I would have to procure. The first examination I had to sit for was the English Learning Language exam (ELL). This test is to assess the applicant's proficiency in English. It was administered at the American Embassy in India. It did not go well. I struggled with the accent of the American administrator who conducted the test and had misunderstood several of his questions. He rejected my application for a Visa. I was devastated. I had failed. My mother had gone to the Embassy with me and was waiting on the other side of the door for the results. How could I face her? I felt I had let her down. When I came out and told her, she hugged me and tried to console me. I told her, "I'm so sorry. I panicked, and I couldn't give it my best." I felt like an abject failure.

I wasn't certain I could bring this dream to fruition. It felt hopeless. It was already September - and classes for the program I was applying to were scheduled to start in January. I didn't have a lot of time. I also wasn't sure where I could get the money to retest, much less get to America. The test cost 15,000 rupees, which we did not have. We were already barely subsisting. It seemed impossible to come up with that amount of money, especially in such a brief time.

I could tell by the look on my mother's face that she felt our dreams had been shattered. There was no hope. No options. I saw no way out either. I fell into a depression. I sat at home for two weeks, brooding. But one day I realized that I had the choice to give up or try again. I decided to try again.

That night at home, I knelt before my mother and gently took both of her hands in mine. With tears in my eyes, I told her, "Mom, if you trust me, I will do this. I just need you to support me. But I promise you, I will give it everything I have!" I gave her my word that I would prove myself. I would succeed. And I would take care of the family once I had made it. We cried together as she assured me she would do everything in her power to help me.

Even during the direst times, we had never asked any of our relatives for help. Most of the family felt my aspirations to go to America were foolish. They believed I would be better off staying where I was and working in more humble jobs. But my mother swallowed her pride and asked her sister for a loan. Her sister agreed, so I reapplied for the test. It was already the first week of December, so the timeline was tight since classes in the States started in January. The Embassy near us had no testing slots open, and the only open slot was on the third week in December, sixteen hours away. My mother and I made the trip together.

I knew I could not fail this time. Failure was not an option. My life, and the lives of my family were at stake! Desperation is sometimes a more powerful motivator than hope. Merely 'hoping' can sometimes be too passive. I was determined to be successful. I was intimately familiar with physical hunger, but this was a different kind of hunger. It came from deep inside me, fueled by love for my family and a fervent desire to alleviate their pain, poverty and, yes, their hunger.

I would make it happen.

I took the test again and passed. With the loan from my aunt, I left everything and everyone familiar to me and flew to the United States to get my Masters.

Attending classes, while also working fifty to sixty hours a week to survive, was utterly exhausting. It wasn't unusual for me to do a shift in a restaurant, then go work in a cigar store and stock shelves in a store on the same day. And, of course, I did work in a gas station. I was aware that there is a stereotyping of people from India working in gas stations. I sometimes wonder if people who see us in this stereotypical way realize many of us work up to seventy hours a week, while attending school full time - just trying to save our families. It takes hard work, perseverance, and commitment. There were times I was so exhausted I wasn't sure if I could go on. Then I would remember my family, which gave me the strength I needed to continue.

It's been ten years since I nervously left my home and came to the United States. I am now a full-time IT Sales Force Developer. In the last five years I have been able to pay back all the money that was loaned to me, as well as pay off all of my family's debts. I am able to send my family money on a regular basis.

When I think about where I've come from - the poverty; the hunger; the lack of opportunity - to where I am now, I am profoundly humbled. Thousands of years ago, Plato stated, 'The true creator is necessity, who is the mother of our invention.' For me, it was necessary to do whatever I could to take care of my family. That necessity generated determination. Applying that determination to hard, consistent work brought success. That success created hope for my future, and the future of my family.

We can't always depend on a wisp of hope and a dream. Sometimes we have to give hope a push.

Jay

"But I know, somehow, that only when it is dark enough can you see the stars."

Martin Luther King, Jr.

A Lesson of Hope

You never know what the next moment may bring.

I was reminded of this a number of years ago by a cat. My husband, Richard, and I were just recovering from the grief of losing the last of our two beloved cats six months earlier. The house felt empty without the sonorous purring, the shameless demands for attention and the speedy appearance at the sound of the can opener. They had both brought such joy and a sense of play into our home. We missed them. We had talked about getting a couple of kittens but had decided to wait a while.

I knew something was wrong when Richard walked in the door one day, yelling - "There is a starving cat out here and I'm going to feed it – I don't care if it comes back!" This was out of character for him. His more typical approach was more akin to, "There is a stray cat outside. Please don't feed it. I don't want a stray cat hanging around here." I got up to see what was eliciting so much fervor. I found a barely alive, emaciated cat just outside our door. I had never seen an animal so wasted. She was literally skin draped over bones. I could see every rib, vertebrae, and bone in her gaunt little body. She could barely stand, and her entire body shook violently with the effort of each step she attempted. I don't think she would have lived through the night without intervention.

There was no question but that we would drop everything and take her to the animal emergency clinic to be checked out by a veterinarian. We wanted to get her whatever help she needed because she was obviously suffering. We also wanted to find out if her condition was disease related, or because she was starving to death. It turned out that she was in great health - she just needed food, water, and a warm place to rest her head.

Since she had already stolen our hearts, it was an easy decision to make her part of our family. We named her Ruth.

The following day I was petting her, as she slept peacefully, her small body nestled on my lap. Her eyes were softly closed, a look of complete ecstasy on her tiny face. Suddenly, I was struck by the realization that just the day before she had been dying of starvation, with no reason to hope her plight would change. After all, how long must she have struggled to be so wasted and near death? There had been no reason to believe her circumstances would suddenly change. And yet, that is exactly what happened. Now, just one day later, she had a family who loved her; she had all the food she could eat; she had a home, safety, and medical care. Her life had instantaneously and unexpectedly been transformed.

A month after Ruth showed up on our doorstep, she had gone from a mere four pounds to twice that weight. She had to have some loose, rotted teeth, caused by severe malnutrition, pulled. After that she was able to eat without pain. In the next few weeks, her filthy, matted and bug infested fur transformed into one that was soft, healthy, and luxurious. Her purr grew louder and more frequent.

She was content – and so too were we.

Ruth's story still moves me deeply. It reminds me of how hopeless it can seem when we are faced with adversity - especially if it continues for a long time. At times, it can feel like our efforts to make positive changes might be for nothing. Yet oftentimes something still drives us to keep searching for help and answers - much like Ruth dragging her emaciated body onto our porch in search of help. Sometimes there appears to be no obvious reason to hope, but just because we can't see a reason doesn't mean there isn't one. Ruth reminds me that there is always a place for hope.

Ruth passed away a few years ago at a ripe old age. She brought a lot of love and joy into our home. We will always be grateful that she chose our house to come to for help.

I still miss Ruth, but I carry a part of her with me. Every time I think of her, I'm reminded of the power of hope, because you never know what the next moment might bring.

Rewritten/edited story originally published by Dr. Diane Gross in Natural Triad Magazine, 2011.

"One should . . . be able to see things as hopeless and yet be determined to make them otherwise."

F. Scott Fitzgerald

Saving Myself

Not so fun fact - 1 in 10 children are sexually abused and 1 in 5 women are sexually assaulted here in the United States. This is a heartbreaking reality that I unfortunately lived.

My mother started dating my abuser, even moving him into the house, before I started school. I have very vivid memories of him sneaking into my bedroom while my brother slept on the top bunk. The abuse progressed over time. I was being groomed to think this was normal. I remember both him and my mom having the "beware of people" talk. The gaslighting to make me believe he wasn't the person they were warning me about was unbelievable.

He decided to re-enlist in the military, so they got married and we moved. The abuse continued, but now that they were married the verbal and physical abuse started. And now, we were hours away from everyone we knew. My brother stayed over at his friend's house often, and my mother worked nights, leaving me alone with him. This is when the abused progressed to rape. This is when I realized what was happening was not normal. His anger became violent to the point of holding me by my throat in the air, screaming in my face until the blood vessels in his eyes burst.

He was stationed in Tennessee, so we moved even further away from family. His drinking, and what we suspect was drug use, became horrendous. He would go on drunken tirades for hours. Anything would set him off. The house had to be perfect; we had to be perfect. And, if we seemed nervous, he would explode. On top of all that, the sexual abuse continued. My mood was starting to shift even at school. I finally told someone about what was happening when I was in fifth grade. Thankfully, she understood the severity and told her parents. Thankfully, her parents called the school. Thankfully, the school was required by law to report. It was all a blur after that.

The walls of our dollhouse began to crumble.

The police showed up, and both my mother and brother were presented with news they never could have imagined. They were blindsided. It was Christmas and, instead of Santa, the police were there. My brother, who is only 18 months older than me, didn't believe it. This was the only father he had ever had. My mom was in denial. She herself was a victim of abuse and couldn't believe she missed the signs.

We were all so far into the world of abuse that we couldn't see a way out of it. I was told by both my mother and my abuser that it was my choice if he stayed or went. My brother had already told me I was the one responsible for our family falling apart - and now I was being put in charge of making this decision. But the police told my abuser he couldn't stay there, so we helped him find an apartment and move. But we would visit him often.

Then he and my mom decided to buy a house before his military loan was unavailable - and he moved back in with us. We drove him to his court hearing in Florida. Our case was handled by the military instead of the state of TN. I wasn't allowed to testify. My mom was afraid they would tear me apart. His sentence was reduced from child rape and molestation to indecent act with a minor. He was sentenced to three years in prison.

He and my mom stayed in contact while he was in prison, and he was released early for good behavior after eighteen months. He moved back in immediately. My grades went from straight A's in advanced classes, to having to drop out of classes for poor grades. He came back angry and bitter about what I had done. My mom told me if I ever felt uncomfortable, I could say so and he would leave. I was told the power was in my hands because I was the victim. He had claimed he must have been so drunk he didn't know what he was doing when he was abusing me - that it wasn't his fault, but it was his responsibility to own what he did.

After a while, I couldn't stand it anymore. He made comments about my body, and tried to bribe me with money to let him touch me. He showed me inappropriate videos and told me stories of his past sex life. I finally got to my breaking point, and told my mom it was time for him to go. She wanted us to go to family counseling with the pastor of our church. He told me God had forgiven my abuser, so I should also. But I still wanted him out.

I couldn't handle the pressure anymore. I called my biological father and asked if I could move in with him. I didn't tell my mom. I just packed all my things, and the day he flew in to pick me up I told her I needed a ride to the airport.

Who I thought was going to save me was no savior. My father had issues of his own. Extreme alcoholism and substance abuse. He would get belligerently drunk or stay up all night obsessively fidgeting, taking apart things and putting them back together. He spent all his money on beer and drugs. He was super controlling and violent. He would throw things at me and try to punch me, screaming at the top of his lungs just for saying I missed my mom and friends. Something as little as a friend calling me would set him off. I didn't last long living there.

After I called the police on him several times, he left me at my uncle's house. He had secretly packed a bag of my things and took off while I was in the bathroom. I stayed with my uncle for a few weeks until my father calmed down enough for me to go back. I think back fondly on the time I stayed with my uncle.

Soon afterwards, I told my dad I was ready to go back to Tennessee. He told me that if I didn't 'shut up and play nice' he would read the details of the DCS (Department of Children's Services) report to everyone I knew - then everyone would know what my abuser had done to me, and know what I was, and what had happened to me. He said he would make sure I never saw my mother again. I told him I would rather live with my stepfather than to live with him. He finally decided I wasn't worth the trouble and sent me home to TN.

When I came back my abuser was angry and spiteful. The court had said we could live together, but he was not allowed to be left alone with me. One morning he came home early because he worked construction and it had started raining. I was in the shower getting ready for school. He kicked the bathroom door in and said, "I'm home, so get out." I stood outside, in the rain, in a towel, until he was ready to leave. The other kids in the neighborhood saw me as they walked past me on their way to the bus stop. I was out there for hours.

My brother wanted nothing to do with me. He had told me, "If you are looking for a father figure and for someone to protect you, don't look at me. You are not my responsibility." He had instructed his friends not to talk to me. He didn't even like people to know we were related. We fought all the time. Our stepfather was OCD, and the house had to be immaculate -which was almost impossible to do. My mother worked all the time; my brother didn't care; and we had five dogs, two cats and a ferret. The responsibility to have the house in order by the time my stepfather got home was on me. It was my responsibility to make sure my brother did his chores. It was also my responsibility to make sure he was up and ready for school. This didn't help our relationship. He wasn't fond of me, his younger sister, acting as if I was his mom. But it was life or death at this point. If our stepfather came home to a messy house, he would go off the rails. I was afraid that one day he was going to go too far.

One morning my stepfather busted into my brother's room, screaming about a belt my brother had borrowed. When my stepfather found out it had been left at a friend's house, he started beating my brother. My six-foot-tall brother was in a ball on the floor as he was being hit over and over. That was my mom's breaking point.

She told my stepfather it was over. He needed to move out. He stayed for a month or so after that. I remember him looking into my eyes and saying, "Guess you aren't getting a Christmas, because I'm taking the money to get a place to live." He couldn't take his pets with him, so after he moved out, he would frequently come to visit the dogs.

My mom started working all the time. She worked twelve-hour shifts at the hospital. With extra shifts and overtime, she often worked ninety-plus hours a week. She also started dating a new guy. Thankfully, this man was able to get rid of the dogs, so my abuser didn't have a reason to come around anymore.

I started having health problems due to all the stress. I was assigned a presentation in school on how to check for predators in your area. My address was on the sex offender's registry list that I had to present in front of my class. I had my first of many seizures that day. I collapsed in front of the class and didn't come-to until I was in the ambulance on the way to the hospital. I continued to have seizures about every two weeks for the next five years. They prescribed me medication for seizures, which didn't stop them, but did cause severe mood swings and hallucinations. So, they prescribed a mood leveler, which made me numb. To this day, I still hate medications. It's hard to get me to even take Tylenol.

My mom was never home, and by that time my brother had moved out. I didn't have many friends because people thought I was a drug addict and crazy because of my health issues. I hated school. I just wanted someone to save me from life. Why did everything have to be so painful? I felt like I had no one, and nowhere to go. One day I came home to an empty house after school and collapsed on the living room floor. I just couldn't do it anymore. I just couldn't take it. I don't think I've ever cried like that before. I let it all out - every single ounce of pain in my body in blood curdling cries. I laid on the living room floor for hours.

After I cried until I couldn't cry anymore, I sat up and cleaned my face. I knew I had been looking in all the wrong places for someone to save me. My mother couldn't, she was a victim of abuse as much as I was. She grew up in abuse and knew nothing else. She did her best with the tools she had. My father had his own demons. He's somewhere in there, but I've still yet to meet him. Maybe one day he'll break free from his addictions, but he wasn't capable of saving me. My brother was a child, he never asked for this responsibility. He was trying to survive our childhood as much as I was. It was unfair to even consider him saving me. The only person who could save me was me. I could choose to continue living through that pain and suffering or I could build a life worth living. I decided to save myself.

I started working, got my license, and as soon as I turned eighteen, I got an apartment. I worked full-time and went to high school full-time. My grades weren't great, and I barely graduated, but I did it.

I remember being told by a court appointed counselor that I would never be happy; that I would live walking on eggshells for the rest of my life. They told me I should never have kids because I would inevitably abuse my children. I was told you can't stop generational trauma, and that 'hurt people hurt people.' Many family members told me not to talk about my abuse, to not air out my dirty laundry. I was told by my mother that I was good, despite her.

They were all wrong.

I am not my abuse. My happiness isn't controlled by my past. I have the option to heal and not be defined by what happened to me. I am not airing my dirty laundry because it's not my dirty laundry. It isn't something I'm ashamed of, these things happened to me. I'm not interested in protecting my abusers by staying silent. What is kept in the dark will fester, but once brought to the light it won't survive. I didn't have the choice or the ability to control what happened to me then - but I do now.

I'm not good despite my mom, I'm good despite my abusers. My mom, my brother, and I survived together. Generational abuse is a hard pattern to break, we just have to do the work.

I speak about my past often. The guilt, shame, and anger have melted away over the years. The seizures stopped too. Through saving myself, I can inspire and provide hope for others that they can do the same.

Liz Tucker

" I don't think of all the misery, but of the beauty that still remains."

Anne Frank

WHERE MAGIC LIVES

A shrouded place
where magic lives;
shimmer of pearls,
a butterfly's birth,
and diamonds form
in ebon earth.

An unlit world
where life begins.
Roots shoot down
in velvet black,
ere reaching up,
light's hope to grasp.

When grief descends,
consumes our world,
the cords of pain
will guide the way
to light unseen
where insight dwells

in darks' caress.
with shuttered eyes,
look deep within
where grief reveals
what matters most:
the light of love.

Diane Gross

"When you can't fly then run, if you can't run then walk, if you can't walk then crawl, but whatever you do, you have to keep moving forward."

Martin Luther King, Jr.

Proof In The Mirror

The feeling that all hope is gone washes over me like a wave.
It's difficult to see past the despair, disappointment and darkness that is
right in front of me.

The feeling is so strong it is almost unbearable:

It's a palpable darkness that obscures hope. There are no cracks
of light, no promise of a new dawn.

It's seductive. It beguiles me with the false promise that to give
up would lead to peace.

It's affirming. It echoes our secret belief that we deserve the
shame, embarrassment, disgust, and failure we are experiencing.

It's overwhelming. The enormity and number of the negative
thoughts flood in like a tsunami.

It's achingly familiar. We've been here before, old friend,
constant companion, hidden secret.

It's deceptive. But it feels like the truest truth of all. It's hard to check the facts and gain perspective when the wave washes over me.

What IS the point?

Disappointment is the worst! It hits hard, in my throat.

When the wave of hopelessness crashes over me, I feel like I am suffocating. I feel paralyzed and unable to move. I struggle to talk or listen, which is ironic since my mind is racing a mile a minute.

When I feel this despair, I need to cry to get rid of some of the cortisol stress hormone that rages through my body. I know I need to breathe and wait for the feeling to pass, but my body doesn't seem able to respond. I have difficulty assessing the passage of time, as well as finding space between thought and action.

I have only recently accepted the proof that 'this too shall pass.' The proof looks at me in the mirror every day. It has taken me 50 years to come to that realization.

The proof? I'm still here!

I do wish, however, that I had come to this realization much earlier in life.

Fear of rejection is a huge fear of mine. I hate, for example, calling people on the phone!

What if they are not there?

What if they are busy?

What if I fumble my words?

I love texting, but, if people don't reply quickly, I start to feel nervous. I tend to read motive into their delayed response. All this fuels my negative, well-rehearsed self-talk script that often runs in the background of my mind. I've noticed I tend to correlate my worth with the speed with which they respond.

Worrisome thoughts spring unbidden to my mind!

They know it's me and they are avoiding me.

Why would anyone want to hear from me anyway?

You talk too much, Janet!

They read my text! Why aren't they replying?

I shouldn't have sent that text! Argh!

In my worst moments I am deeply sad to feel so completely alone in the world. I now recognize that I have long held a fear of being alone. I tried to hide that fear by trying to fill the loneliness with people, drugs, alcohol, and even work. I took every opportunity to fill the void and avoid sitting with it.

I identify as confused and uncomfortable. I feel like I missed those days in school when they told everyone the important stuff, like how to make friends; how to set healthy boundaries, how to label and process my feelings, how to say 'no,' and how to be kind to myself.

Other people seem mysterious and... perfect. How are they all able to live without crushing self-doubt? Why doesn't everyone else question everything?

Socializing used to seem easy, but a lot of alcohol was typically involved.

Now, I don't drink much, nor do I have the energy to socialize. Sometimes I wonder if I am isolating myself more and more - or am I setting good boundaries? Am I becoming a hermit, or am learning to take more time for self-care? I'm not sure that I have a clear answer yet, but maybe it is a combination of both. I am, however, learning to enjoy the journey.

Today, in 2024, I am equal parts embarrassed and proud of myself. I'm embarrassed that it has taken so damn long to figure it out, but I'm also proud that I can at least recognize the slippery slope - even if only when I am falling.

I'm working toward the time when pride will override and overtake embarrassment.

It's funny how even talking about feeling proud of myself ignites shame...

I have begun to put into practice some wisdom I have heard for 50 years about things that can help maintain physical and emotional balance. Ignoring the needs of the body and mind can trigger feelings of hopelessness, embarrassment, and shame. We all need sufficient sleep, nourishing food, movement, and compassionate self-talk to experience health in every area of our lives, including emotional health. I have begun to see ever more clearly that when I neglect these things, I pay the price!

The past 5 years have been the worst. I have felt broken, defeated, hopeless and uncomfortable.

I know that the process of breaking has allowed me to see all the parts of myself more clearly. I believe this has been a necessary process:

break into pieces.
examine the broken pieces.
accept the brokenness and myself.
prioritize and discard what no longer works or fits
polish and reassemble.
learn and move forward.

I'm learning to love all the pieces of me!

When the student (me) is ready, the teacher (also me) will appear.

I am learning to practice radical acceptance. If I 'fall,' I try to honor that I did the best I could with what I had, and I acknowledge that some days my resources were low.

I have placed a note on my bathroom mirror that says, "I am going to look after you today" (inspired by Kristin Neff*). That reminds me that I am deserving of my own love and tender care.

At this time of my life, I am almost comfortable being uncomfortable. I am less inclined to turn on myself in a way that beats me down. It reminds me of the words of Andrea Gibson, "Beating yourself up is never a fair fight."

I'm still here. I'm growing, learning to love myself more deeply and committed to continue walking a healing path.

And now, as I sit here in the sun, as spring approaches, I feel a bit of hope!

Janet Lawson

Without The Sadness

I said, "I don't know who I am without the sadness."

Without the heaviness. Without the pain.
Without the rainy skies and the heartache.
Without the nightmares and the terrors.

The sadness is an old pair of jeans
 that is worn in all the right places.
Old sneakers, just starting to fray,
the laces knotted in too many places.

And the sadness is also gone.
There is an empty space on the bookshelf of me
where the book of sadness used to be.
There's a sticky note that says "it used to be here"
but when I reach for the familiar pages
my fingers touch nothing but sunlight in the empty space.

I said, "I don't know who I am without the sadness."

And the love of my life held my cheeks in his hands,
ocean blue eyes peering into my stormy sky blue,
and told me who I am.

Strong.

Kind.

Funny.

Intelligent.

Brave.

Bright.

Joyful.

Beautiful.

"You are loved," he said.

Annie Louise Twitchell

Redemptive Hope

Our conversations with some of the authors in this book, as well as with some who chose not to share their stories at this time, revealed a common thread. Though it wasn't true in every instance, some struggled with feelings of intense self-reproach and deep regret about the past. This wasn't surprising, since most of us have had this experience at some point in our life. This book, however, gave us a very close-up and condensed view of how prevalent regret can be when we view our lives in retrospect. Many looked back at their lives and wished things could have been different. This was true regardless of whether they had caused harm or were the one who had been hurt. Many still felt guilty for the pain they had inflicted on others. Some experienced self-recrimination for times when they were rendered powerless in the face of overwhelming circumstances.

Hope is often viewed as a time specific to the future, but it's far more nuanced. Our relationship with the past can dramatically affect our relationship with the present, as well as the future. People frequently wish they could travel back in time and re-write history. They struggle with the impossible hope for a different and better past. The burden of this lost hope can be extraordinarily heavy. Whether they were harmed, or were the ones who caused harm, an answer to the question some searched for was: When all hope is gone for a different and better past - what then?

Listening to and reading the stories of these remarkable people during the writing of this book provided us with a bird's eye view of their incredible courage and resilience. It made us more deeply cognizant of the fact that we often are not privy to the unseen histories of people that influence and drive their choices. Suffering from trauma, lack of education, early exposure to drugs and alcohol, as well as poverty and hunger are sometimes factors, all of which can be profoundly impactful. Sometimes these earlier influences led to poor choices and unhealthy ways of interacting as adults. Their loved ones sometimes became collateral to their residual trauma responses. Not everyone was driven by previous trauma though. Some we spoke with lived fairly uneventful lives until their world was torn apart by some catastrophic occurrence. But those events also sometimes affected people's ability to respond in ways they would have hoped. These extenuating circumstances matter, because even though our individual histories do not negate issues of personal responsibility and accountability, it does make space for understanding and compassion. It also can illuminate the need for, and role of, healing as a necessary aspect for change.

It also creates an opening for redemptive hope.

Over time, a lot has changed for many of the people with whom we interviewed, and whose stories we read and edited. They have worked hard to heal. They have, through hard work and practice, made permanent and positive changes in their lives. This takes courage and tremendous fortitude. It demands respect.

Still, they often find themselves wishing they could go back and change the past. They would love to rewind the clock and correct their mistakes. Of course, they can't. There is no hope of creating a different and better past. There is only hope to create a better future.

Finding peace by letting go of all hope for a better past doesn't mean we are abdicating responsibility for our previous actions. In fact, quite the opposite. We can regret our mistakes and poor choices, especially the ones that caused others pain, but if we aren't careful, we can begin to torture ourselves for having made those bad choices. The only choices we have control over now are those we make from this moment forward. We can't change the ones we made when we were exhausted, overwhelmed, or terrified. We can't change what we did when 'fight or flight' wasn't even a possibility because we were stuck in survival 'freeze' mode. It's the choices we make now that create hope for transformation - for redemption.

The story, 'A Christmas Carol' is a powerful illustration of redemptive hope. Ebenezer Scrooge was a mean and heartless man, who one night had a redemptive experience. Three visitors came to reveal visions of his past, present and future life. That night changed him to his core. The Ebenezer who emerged from that night's experience was NOT the same Ebenezer who had gone to bed the night before. They were two very different people. The joy and love that emanated from him upon his awakening was palpable and contagious. That positive impact would have been dampened had he ruminated overly much on the guilt of his past rather than the joy and hope he felt on that new morning. He had an emotional and spiritual rebirth.

The person we are now may be a very different person than the person we once were. The path to freedom from self-recrimination is claiming and owning our new birth and personhood. There is hope in forgiveness, especially self-forgiveness. To choose to look at the past and accept that we were flawed, and maybe even broken is humbling. To be honest, the choice to find hope in forgiving ourselves may sometimes feel as if we are minimizing the pain we caused. Sometimes we may feel we don't have the right to be forgiven, much less forgive ourselves. Yet, there is no hope to fully realize our best future if we do anything less.

Editors Dr. Diane Gross and Annie Louise Twitchell

Hope Is The Thing With Feathers

Hope is the thing with feathers

That perches in the soul,

And sings the tune without the words,

And never stops at all,

And the sweetest in the gale is heard;

And sore must be the storm

That could abash the little bird

That kept so many warm.

I've heard it in the chilliest land,

And on the strangest sea;

Yet, never, in extremity,

It asked a crumb of me.

Emily Dickenson, 1891

ABOUT THE EDITORS

Dr. Diane Gross is a Doctor of Oriental Medicine, Licensed Acupuncturist and Holistic Life Coach who specializes in treating physical and emotional pain. While she has been privileged to help others on their healing path, she also continues to do her own healing work. Having grown up in an abusive home environment, she is intimately familiar with pain – both physical and emotional. Like many who practice the healing arts, she recognizes that she is essentially 'a wounded healer.' Being entrusted to read and edit the stories in this book has been an honor of a lifetime. She believes sharing our stories helps us heal, connect and learn from one another.

Annie Louise Twitchell is a writer, editor, photographer, and first responder who lives and works in Rural Maine. Ever since she was a young child, she has wanted to help people; her work in emergency medical services and in writing allow her to have a wide impact and to help a broad community. Being invited to work with this collection of stories has been one of the great joys of her career.

Made in the USA
Monee, IL
08 September 2025

25268454R00125